REDISCOVERING
THE ROLE OF THE
CHURCH

GOD'S GOVERNMENT ON EARTH

ANDREW DARRAH

ARK house

Ark House Press
arkhousepress.com

Unless otherwise identified, Scripture quotations are taken from the HOLY BIBLE, NEW INTERNATIONAL VERSION, Copyright 1973, 1978, 1984, 2010. International Bible Society. All rights reserved.

Cataloguing in Publication Data:
Title: Rediscovering the Role of The Church: God's Government on Earth
ISBN: 978-0-6454117-0-6 (pbk)
Other Authors/Contributors: Darrah, Andrew;

Typeset by initiateagency.com

CONTENTS

ACKNOWLEDGEMENTS

All glory goes to my Lord and King, Jesus Christ. There is not a paragraph in this book that is not inspired by His Holy Spirit. I could not have put this book together without Him.

"Houses and wealth are inherited from parents, but a prudent wife is from the LORD" (Proverbs 19:14). I want to express my gratitude to my God-given, beautiful wife Margaret for all her love and support over the years. I could not ask for a better mother for Caleb, my son. I dearly love and cherish you both. This achievement is yours too, because it would not be possible without your corporate effort.

I call myself blessed because I have a wonderful family I can count on. Special thanks to my dear parents for laying a foundation for me through their hard work and sacrifice, and to the rest of the family for their love over the years.

DEDICATION

Just two months before his death, I had the opportunity not only to meet him but to receive his blessing. I believe his ministry laid the foundation for mine. Special dedication to my spiritual father, the late Dr Myles Monroe. You were a blessing not only to me but to our entire generation. Your act of obedience to the call of God and dedication to the message of the Kingdom of God is my motivation for this book. It is always a blessing to read your books and listen to your Spirit-inspired teachings.

Also to all truth seekers, especially my beloved brothers and sisters in Christ who are seeking to serve God better by aligning with His major will and purpose for the earth.

A special dedication to the youth all over the world who have been disillusioned and left confused by all the various religions that promise to have answers to life but do not deliver.

And finally, to all young people who have a call to ministry.

PREFACE

Nothing is probably worse than a teenager who has to deal with no sense of meaning and purpose in life and the doubts associated with being born into a religious family. I had to attend the Sunday services, and whether I felt like it or not, join in the worship and praise, as well as hear the long, often boring sermons, and pay my way out of the attendance by means of the offerings collected. Church meant nothing more to me than an activity that stole my time from my favorite television show, which happened to be on at the same time as the services. I could not identify with the Church, because I felt it was not relevant to the issues I was dealing with then. Of course there is the promise of heaven, and that was good to know, but I was naively confident I would live long enough to make the necessary changes in my life required to make it to heaven before I died. The promise of heaven was not enough for me to take church seriously as a teenager. I was on the search for relevance, and Christianity was just too future-oriented for me to identify with.

In my mid-to-late twenties, I started noticing a change in my long-forsaken religion. The sermons were becoming more relevant to me. Some preachers echoed the Personal Development and Motivational speakers I listened to. They taught biblical principles that were life applicable. This switch rekindled my interest in the Church again, but the excitement was short lived when the so called "prosperity gospel" became the focus of most preachers. I was far from being "holy" by any standard, but I had heard the story of Jesus countless times as a child and knew Jesus stood for more than just a seed-sowing and harvest-reaping prosperity gospel. I again turned a blind eye to the Church and continued to look to the world for answers. While learning, conniving, and striving to play by the rules of the systems of the world, I had a dramatic encounter with God. Little did I know that it would mark the end of a meaningless life of confusion and struggles and open a new chapter of a life dedicated to seeking and serving God in truth.

In the year 2013, I literally understood what it meant to be "sitting on a fence." Australia was back to the polls again for the elections. As a nonbeliever in the past, I had no issues at all when voting in the previous years.

This time, being a born-again, Spirit-filled, devoted believer, I was determined to endorse the party whose policies and leader portrayed values and principles of God. There were two major parties presenting different policies, but that still didn't make my decision any easier.

My quest for a political party with policies founded on God's Word and a born-again, devoted believer leader, got me "sitting on the fence." None of the parties were totally committed to the principles and values of God. In the end, I had to settle for the party and leader that represented more of those principles and values. I was disappointed because my choice was not a true reflection of what I wanted, but it was the only option I had, knowing that I was obligated by the Australian constitution to vote, being an Australian citizen.

I believe many Christians or believers have encountered similar situations. For example, we are often presented leaders that on the positive, for example, may be against abortion. However, they may support sending troops overseas during conflicts to engage in operations that kill civilians, including children. The truth is, sometimes we wish some of our selfless, God-loving, devoted pastors would run for the elections so that our voting experience would be much more enjoyable. But what if believers or Christians already have a political leader who portrays the values we believe in, such as love, peace, justice, mercy, goodness, gentleness, unity, compassion, and holiness? What if we did not have to settle for hypocritical leaders that believe in control, division, manipulation, greed, revenge, selfishness, power, and corruption?

I came to the realization that God wanted to use me to address the very questions I had asked myself several times as a teenager. "What is the relevance and the role of the Church in our societies and the world at large?"

Of course, others may have their own answers to this question; I am not here to only give you my answer, but to present to you what I believe is my God-given life purpose on earth.

In this book, I will be discussing truths that are concealed or often ignored. Truths that the world may not be able to accept, and yet the very truths that will set humanity free from all our struggles.

FOREWORD

Have you ever wondered which church is the right church? Why are there many churches out there claiming to be the right ones and insisting that the others are wrong? Why are there many people having passion for the church, while others are stumbling and leaving their faith because of the church?! As Christians, we might all agree on the heart of Christianity, which is the salvation work of our Lord and saviour, Jesus Christ. That's why we all share the same sign of the cross. When it comes to the cross, there is unity. However, when it comes to the church, that's where the division takes place.

In this book, Andrew Darrah boldly addresses the issue of the Church—not from any denominational perspective, but from the Kingdom of God foundational view.

I have read many books before, not only as a publisher, but as a passionate reader and I have never been revolutionised by the subject of the Church as I have been with this one. I have always been passionate about the church since I was a young boy. I always loved the church and always loved spending time serving in the church. But I also had this question inside me: "What does the perfect church look like?!"

The moment I laid my eyes on the manuscript title, which included the words "God's Government on Earth," I thought the answer will be there. I started reading the book and I couldn't stop; I finished the whole manuscript in one day. Andrew is not displaying his point of view to educate readers with a new concept, but he gives a complete scriptural basis for what the Holy Spirit revealed about a Church after God's own heart. He is basically rediscovering the role of the church that was lost during the ages, due to many factors and especially culture. He shows us a church where Jesus is the King and the operations are governed by the major Kingdom principle of love. This is a church that displays God's kingdom culture where the Holy Spirit is the Governor and the citizens are God's family.

We are living in a very exciting yet critical season in history. We are in a season where the whole creation groans eagerly, expecting the children of God to be revealed (Romans 8:19). The only hope this world currently has is in Jesus. He wants to penetrate the increasing darkness around us with a Church that lives by the Kingdom Government of heaven.

The church described in this book is the image of the beautiful Bride the Lord is revealing in these end times to prepare for His coming. It is time for all of the body of Christ, and especially church leaders, not only to learn and teach but to apply the principles of God's Kingdom government outlined in this book. I am confident that the teachings and principles Andrew has shared, along with the guidance of the Holy Spirit, will greatly contribute to the emergence of a shift in the church culture—as well as the rise of faithful servants passionate about enforcing God's Kingdom government on earth, as it is in Heaven.

Sherif Farag
CEO – The Word Group
Print | Publishers | Media

INTRODUCTION

Please permit me to begin with an old religious farce, which I believe portrays the subject of this book.

The Lord spoke to Noah and said:

"In six months I am going to make it rain until the whole world is covered with water and all the evil things are destroyed. But I want to save a few good people and two of every living thing on the planet. I am ordering you to build an ark." And in a flash of lightning, he delivered the specifications for the ark. *"Okay,"* Noah said, trembling with fear and fumbling with the blueprints, *"I'm your man."*

Six months passed, the sky began to cloud up, and the rain began to fall in torrents. The Lord looked down and saw Noah sitting in his yard, weeping, and there was no ark.

"Noah!" shouted the Lord. "Where is my ark?" A lightning bolt crashed into the ground right beside Noah. *"Lord, please forgive me!"* begged Noah. *"I did my best, but there were some big problems. First,*

I had to get a building permit for the ark's construction, but your plans did not meet their code.

"Then I had a big problem getting enough wood for the ark because there was a ban on cutting trees to save the spotted owl. I tried to convince the environmentalists and the U.S. Fish and Wildlife Service that I needed the wood to save the owls, but they wouldn't let me catch them, so no owls.

"Next I started gathering up the animals but got sued by an animal rights group that objected to me taking along only two of each kind. Just when the suit got dismissed, the EPA notified me that I couldn't complete the ark without filling out an environmental impact statement on your proposed flood. They didn't take kindly to the idea that they had no jurisdiction over the Supreme Being. Really, I don't think I can finish the ark in less than five years."

With that, the sky cleared, the sun began to shine, and a rainbow arched across the sky. Noah looked up and smiled. "You mean you are not going to destroy the world?" he asked hopefully.

"No," said the Lord. "The government already has."

Here is the moral of the joke: God's purposes for the earth are obstructed when the governments on earth are not aligned with His will. This is why the "Lord's Prayer," as taught by Jesus, petitions for God's Kingdom government on earth, so that His "will" will be done on earth as it is in Heaven (see Matt. 6:10).

Society has a way of placing labels on people. For most of us, people around us—whether they are family, friends, schoolmates, work colleagues, etc.—have a matching label they believe perfectly describes who we are. Jesus was perceived as one of the most controversial and misunderstood people of His day, because society then could not come up with any singular label that was perfectly suited to Him. They resorted to identifying Him with all sorts of titles and names, such as prophet, teacher, Elijah, Jeremiah, John the Baptist reincarnated, etc. To add to their confusion, Jesus claimed to be King: the long-anticipated Messiah of the Jews that the prophet Isaiah had spoken of to be bringing "the government" on the earth.

If you have ever wondered why Jesus was not only persecuted by the religious leaders of His days but also by the Roman kingdom government, here is your answer: He was undertaking activities that were deemed religious, but He was proclaiming a new and superior Kingdom government, His own Kingdom. Jesus taught His principles and demonstrated the power of His Kingdom government to followers who later became the Church.

It has often been mistakenly perceived by the world as a building for the gathering of weird folks referred to as Christians, but the Church is the agency for God's practical Kingdom government on earth. It is a government "body," not a religious institution. In other words, God's ordained government authorities in every country on earth are the members of the Church. All legislation and laws that govern our lifestyle on earth must come through the Church sourced from principles taught by King Jesus. That is and has been God's plan all along. It is the reason why Jesus came and the reason for His death and resurrection. Everything God has done, is doing, and is going to do centers on this purpose.

The opposer, or Satan as he is better known, has assigned his agents to delay God's purpose knowing that he cannot stop it. It was not just a mere act of the disobedience of God's Word by the first man (Adam) and woman (Eve); it was also the outright rejection of God's government over their lives on earth. Any form of government on earth that does not acknowledge the sovereignty of God's Word is a representation of man's opposition and rebellion against God's government. It makes no difference whether it is a democratic or communist society as long as man is the decision maker on the governing laws.

It is clear that before His death, Jesus submitted to the authority of the Roman kingdom government of the day (see Joh. 19:11), but after His resurrection, Jesus stated that all authority in heaven and on earth had been given to Him (see Matt. 28:18). This was the turning point. The government and authority of the earth was given to Jesus, and He delegated it to His Church (see Matt 28:19).

It is not a coincidence that some worldly government leaders employ the services of Christian spiritual leaders by seeking their advice or approval on certain issues. Somehow, worldly government authorities know the position and importance of the role of God's Church in the government of the earth. The problem is that worldly governments are not willing to completely hand over the affairs of the earth to the Church. Satan, who sought to be king in heaven, now seeks to maintain his counterfeit kingdom disguised in various forms of government on earth through them.

What I am looking to share and achieve in this book is to explain that Jesus came to institute a new government on earth to fulfill Isaiah's prophecy. It is a superior government that is sourced from Heaven. It functions independently and cannot coexist with any others on earth. It is the Kingdom government of God through the body of Christ or the Church, the agency for the rule and authority of God over all the earth.

Join me in this journey as we explore God's eternal purpose for the earth. We will expose the defects in the worldly governments, and with the help of the Holy Spirit, paint a clear picture of how God's Spiritual Kingdom government is operative through His Church.

WHAT IS GOVERNMENT?

From the homeless man on the street to the rich business owner in the mansion, the word "government" is common to the lips of all. Somehow we know government plays a crucial role in all aspects of our lives; hence we blame all societal dysfunctions and problems on the government. To express our dissatisfaction, we normally accuse governing authorities of being incompetent, corrupt, greedy, power-hungry, and self-serving. The result is civil unrest in nearly all corners of the earth, which can be seen in the form of mass protests often erupting in violence and war. The search for a perfect government is the cause of all national and international tragic conflicts. But what is government?

1

God's Government of Natural Systems

All of you have to do is observe nature and you will realize one truth about God. He is highly orderly. His entire creation is intelligently ordered. The organization of the solar system, ecosystem, and even the complex yet intricately ordered design of the human body, give away a God of precision. Somehow the sun knows to always arise in the east and set in the west; the systems of your body know how to cooperatively function together in an orderly manner for your well-being. These are just a few of the many wonders that confound atheist scientists that have often sought to postulate a "no-God theory."

- *"For God is not a God of disorder but of peace—as in all the congregations of the Lord's people." (1 Cor. 14:33)*

But what entity permits these complex systems of nature to thrive for everything to be done decently and in order? The answer? Government. It is God's in-built instructions or laws in these natural systems that ensure order and efficiency.

The Importance of Government

Government is central to everything in life because government in the right form produces order, structure, stability, peace, protection, prosperity, guidance, health, purpose, and a host of many benefits. Just as all natural systems require government, virtually any entity with more than one person cannot function without proper government. Government is the glue that binds people or processes together. Where there is no proper government, there is confusion and chaos. The book of Judges records a time of chaos in the history of the Israelites when they had no king. The disorder was the direct result of the lack of proper government. *"In those days Israel had no king; everyone did as they saw fit."* *(Judges 21:25)*

The Need for Governing Laws

It is a requirement for any number of people sharing the same space or living together to have laws so that their rights as individuals and as a group are protected to ensure peace and harmony. Our unique personalities necessitate boundaries or governing laws in our relationships. For example, in many families, there may be written or unwritten laws that exist, especially for children. These laws are important for producing peace and order within the family, so that each member can operate effectively in their defined role as a member of the family. In most cases, failure to observe and respect such boundaries is the reason for many broken relationships. Peace is the foundation of prosperity. Because laws are significant for something as important as maintaining peace, there must be a leader(s) responsible for ensuring that each individual complies with the laws.

Definition and Role of Government

Wherever there are people, laws, and leader(s), there is some form of government. Government is simply the control exercised over the actions of the members, citizens, or inhabitants of communities, societies, and states.

Government has two main roles:

- To maintain peace and harmony.

- To orchestrate wise use of available resources to cater to the needs of the people, especially those disadvantaged within the community or state.

These roles performed by government are so crucial that the lack of proper government inevitably breeds injustice, confusion, disorder, war, poverty, diseases and inefficiencies that affect nations, communities, families and individuals. This is why most political campaigns for the seat of government greatly emphasis and promise peace and prosperity to citizens.

Forms of Government

There are various forms of government. There is Republic, Socialism, Monarchy (Kingdom), Democracy, Marxism, Aristocracy, Communism, Totalitarianism, etc. But I will briefly explain the three forms that are most prevalent in our modern contemporary society and that are relevant to the theme of this book.

Democratic Government

Democracy is the most common form of government in our modern contemporary society. It originated from "ancient" Greece. The Greeks have a history of an era when they believed life started and ended with humans. It was known as the age of "reason". They had little or no regard for the Most High God and basically made a "god" of their own intellect and reason. Consequently, they invented a form of government that would allow men to "reason" out and decide on the governing laws of their lives and elect leaders or officials by majority votes of the citizens. Democracy is simply the government of the people by the people. It is the rule of law decided on and passed by the majority votes of citizens.

The Economic Structure of Democracy

The economic structure of this form of government is known as Capitalism. There are compulsory income deductions (taxes) by the government to support the community; however, this system is still not designed for the common good of the community of people. Capitalism greatly emphasizes personal pursuit and individual success. It inevitably creates a society with an uneven distribution of wealth. A common phrase in this form of government is "the Haves" and "the Have Nots." The result is rampant competition, greed, fear, worry, competition, jealousy, envy, poverty, strife, prevalent in democratic societies.

How a Democratic Government Would Work in Your Family

Let me apply this system of government on a small scale to the human family for clarity on its operation. It would mean equal rights for father, mother, and children. Therefore, in the case where there are more children in the family, by majority votes, the children can have some laws passed and implemented for their parents to comply with; or worse still, a child could be elected to lead the family. The great emphasis on individual responsibility would also mean that besides obligatory contributions from each member of the family for the common good, the family does not have to support each other if they don't want to. The father is not obligated to provide for his family, even if he has the capacity to do so.

Communist Government

Communism is a system of government pioneered by a man who also happened to be a humanist. Like the Greeks, Karl Marx had little or no regard for God, so again his invention places man in the center of government. A communist differs from a democratic society in that even though the people may elect the leaders, the appointed leaders decide the governing laws.

The Economic Structure of Communism

The economic structure of this form of government is designed to suit the community as a whole, but at the expense of individual rights. The wealth of individuals is compulsorily shared amongst the community of people. All property belongs to the state. There are no private ownership rights in this system of government.

How a Communist Government
Would Work in Your Family

A small-scale application of this form of government to the human family would mean that a child could be appointed the leader and would have the responsibility of making and enforcing family rules. Also, members of the family would have no individual ownership rights. The whole family shares all individual gains.

Kingdom (Monarchy) Government

A kingdom government is a very different system from the two forms described above. In a kingdom, a king owns all property, including the people living in the country/territory. The king therefore holds the sole responsibility for making and enforcing all governing laws, as well as making all necessary provisions for the community of people. Unlike Democracy or Communism, citizens in a kingdom do not get to vote on who they want as leader or decide on any governing laws.

The Economic Structure of a Kingdom

A Kingdom operates on a principle of access. Citizens have access to everything but own nothing because the king, who is also Lord, owns everything. The king has the sole responsibility of catering to the needs of all the citizens in his territory; therefore, the wealth in a kingdom is common to all. "Commonwealth" is the economic system in a kingdom. The distinctive mark of a kingdom is that the only responsibility of the citizens is to obey the king, and the king, on the other hand, has the duty to make all necessary provisions for his people.

How a Kingdom Government Would Work in Your Family

From a biblical and most cultural standpoint, the human family is an example of a kingdom government. It is the joy of every parent to have well-trained children that grow up to be responsible adults. This goal is only achievable through the control exercised in a kingdom government where the parents, acknowledged as source and providers, make and enforce all the major family laws or rules that would ensure the desired outcome.

If God is our Father and we are His children as the Bible states, only a Kingdom government can exist in the family relationship. *"Follow God's example, therefore, as dearly loved children"(Eph. 5:2)*. You can see why Jesus often made statements like:

- *But I tell you, love your enemies and pray for those who persecute you, **that you may be children of your Father in heaven**. He causes his sun to rise on the evil and the good, and sends rain on the righteous and the unrighteous. (Matt. 5:44–45)*

- *Be perfect, therefore, as your heavenly Father is perfect. (Matt. 5:48)*

Is God Interested in Government?

Why would a Spiritual God be interested in a practical government of humans on earth? My answer to that is: if God is interested in your life, then He has to be interested in the government that oversees your life here on earth. You may not be aware, but laws passed by the government influence communities, families, and individual lives. Bear in mind that individuals constitute families that make up communities and form nations that are subject to laws passed by the government.

For example, most western countries have a law passed against disciplining a child with a rod when the Bible clearly commands, *"Do not withhold discipline from a child; if you punish them with the rod, they will not die. Punish them with the rod and save them from death." (Proverbs 23:13–14)*

In this situation, the role of parents as given by God is restrained by the worldly governments; therefore, God's will concerning the development of children is impaired. I personally believe this contrary law largely contributes to the violence, crime, theft, and many immoral behaviors in our societies.

I hope you have been able to grasp in this opening chapter the importance and impact of government in our lives and why we need God's government in the lives of individuals, families, communities, nations, and the whole earth.

Which Form of Government Will Depict God's Own Government?

If God is interested in government of the earth, which one out of the three forms of government described will depict His form of government? Will it be a democratic government, which is founded on majority votes on laws and leaders by men OR a communist government that also centers on opinions, decisions, and laws of men?

It is only logical that the creator, author, and designer of life, one who rightfully owns everything on this earth, adopts a Kingdom system of government—which acknowledges Him as the source of all provisions, and therefore allows Him the rights to make and enforce all governing laws of our lives.

As I previously stated, wherever there are people, laws, and leader(s), there is some form of government. If worldly governments, whether a democratic or communist society, are made up of people living by man-made laws, then God's government is simply God's people living by God's will or laws. Does this sound like a description of the body of believers (the Church)?

Key Statements

- Wherever there are people, laws, and leader(s), there is some form of government.

- A government is simply the control exercised over the actions of the members, citizens, or inhabitants of communities, societies, and states.

- Government is central to everything in life because government in the right form produces order, structure, stability, peace, protection, prosperity, guidance, health, purpose, and a host of many benefits.

- God's in-built instructions or laws in natural systems are those that ensure order and efficiency.

- Where there is no proper government, there is confusion and chaos.

- The search for a perfect government is the cause of all national and international tragic conflicts.

- If God is our Father and we are His children as the Bible states, only a Kingdom government can exist in the family relationship.

- It is only logical that the creator, author, and designer of life, one who rightfully owns everything on this earth, adopts a Kingdom system of government—which acknowledges Him as the source of all provisions, and therefore allows Him the rights to make and enforce all governing laws of our lives.

God's Plan From
The Beginning

When the Pharisees questioned Jesus on the issue of divorce, Jesus referenced the book of Genesis to reveal God's original purpose or intent regarding that subject matter (see Matt 19:3). This shows that God's purposes from the beginning do not and have not changed. Every major and final biblical truth, therefore, is stated in the book of Genesis.

God's motivation for the creation of Adam and Eve is common to all 7 billion people on earth at present, because we are their descendants. We can deduce how God wants to relate to us now by how He related to them.

Before the Creation of Man

In the books by God's prophets, Ezekiel (chap. 28) and Isaiah (chap. 14), we become aware that before the creation of man, God had already created myriads of angels. These angelic beings were created to do God's will and express His glory and majesty. Lucifer, meaning "the shining one" was a chief archangel placed in charge of many angels and led them in worship to God.

The Bible recounts that Lucifer led one-third of the angels in rebellion against God with the aim of establishing his own rival kingdom. God overpowered his rebellion, and Lucifer with his angels were expelled from heaven.

Lucifer became known as Satan (the adversary) and occupied the earth.

- *How you have fallen from heaven, morning star, son of the dawn! You have been cast down to the earth, you who once laid low the nations! You said in your heart, "I will ascend to the heavens; I will raise my throne above the stars of God; I will sit enthroned on the mount of assembly, on the utmost heights of Mount Zaphon. I will ascend above the tops of the clouds; I will make myself like the Most High. (Is. 14:12–14)*

The Creation of Man

We read in the book of Genesis (chap. 1) that when God approached the earth it was formless, void, had no life, and was filled with darkness. This was probably due to Satan and his angels' occupancy. Since God owns all creation, including the earth, He invaded the earth and began to recycle and restructure it for His new created being called man. Adam was created in the image and likeness of God and was endowed with power to dominate all the rest of God's creation, operating above the forces of Satan that already existed on earth.

- So God created mankind in his own image, in the image of God he created them; male and female he created them. God blessed them and said to them, *"Be fruitful and increase in number; fill the earth and subdue it. Rule over the fish in the sea and the birds in the sky and over every living creature that moves on the ground." (Gen. 1:27–28)*

God did this to demonstrate His greater glory in a lesser being (Man) and advance His Kingdom government of Heaven to the earth, which Satan and his angels had occupied. God's plan was to work through man only as man was submitted to Him. In essence, man was created to govern the earth in the likeness (nature) of God. God is His Word, so God's likeness (nature) is simply God's Word. Put another way, Man was created by God to govern the earth but within the confines of God's sovereign and dominating Word.

God's Kingship Revealed

- The LORD God took the man and put him in the Garden of Eden to work it and take care of it. And the LORD God commanded the man, *"You are free to eat from any tree in the garden; but you must not eat from the tree of the knowledge of good and evil, for when you eat from it you will certainly die."* (Gen. 2:15–17)

These acts of God in the above Scripture are not only Father-like but that of a King and Lord. Note that God put His created man (Adam) in the garden, instructed him to keep it, and gave him access to all food except the tree of the knowledge of good and evil. As I briefly explained in the previous chapter, in a kingdom, the king owns the people and everything in the territory, so he makes and enforces all governing laws that are to be obeyed by the citizens and also makes all necessary provisions for them.

The Fall of Man

God, however, gave man a choice between following our own "will" (self- government) and doing His will (submitting to His Kingdom government). While God's will (Kingdom government) has superiority over satanic power, Man's own will (self-government) falls under the influence of Satan's power. But Man (Adam and Eve) chose against God's will so the Kingdom government of God with its superior power was recalled by God.

Man's "will" (self-government) automatically fell under the force and control of the power of Satan and his angels that already existed on the earth.

The Key Principle of a Kingdom Government

I spent most of my childhood moving from relative to relative because my parents had travelled offshore seeking greener pastures. Every place I settled had its own set of rules and regulations I had to comply with. By the time I was a teenager, the last thing I wanted was to be tied down by rules. I despised authority in any form, but my father did not hesitate to rise against and condemn that behavior when I finally got to live with him. There was a statement he made every time I tried to push the boundaries he had set for me. He'd say, "As long as you are living in my house, you will do what I say. If you cannot comply with my rules, then move out of my house." I am sure many of us have heard our parents make such statements. Well, I don't think there could a better illustration to explain God's relationship to us, being that He is not only our Father but also a King. God's Kingship means that any form of rebellion against His authority purports disconnection from His provisions.

When Adam and Eve disobeyed God's Word, they lost access to God's provisions for them. They instantly lost their role as vice governors of the earth and were expelled from the garden, which had the influence of God's Kingdom government.

- *So the Lord God banished him from the Garden of Eden to work the ground from which he had been taken. After he drove the man out, he placed on the east side of the Garden of Eden cherubim and a flaming sword flashing back and forth to guard the way to the tree of life. (Gen. 3:23-24)*

Man Becomes a Victim in His Own Environment

Man became a victim of the very things we were created to dominate, and until today, disobedience to God's Word or the rebellion against His Kingdom government *is the cause* of confusion, war, stress, diseases, poverty and so-called "natural disasters."

God's Word is Spirit and has complete dominion in both the spiritual and natural realm. Failure to operate in His Word (likeness) is to be dominated by other forces. The ability to dominate and control circumstances on earth is only possible under God's Kingdom government through His sovereign Word.

- *The Spirit gives life; the flesh counts for nothing. The words I have spoken to you—they are full of the Spirit and life. (John 6:63)*

God's Motivation for the Creation of Man

We can agree that God's purpose since the beginning is to get people in His image and likeness (Adam and Eve before the fall) to govern the earth with His sovereign Word (God's Kingdom government). It is evident that God will take His property (the earth) from people that are rebellious to His rule.

- *"If he did not spare the ancient world when he brought the flood on its ungodly people, but protected Noah, a preacher of righteousness, and seven others; if he condemned the cities of Sodom and Gomorrah by burning them to ashes, and made them an example of what is going to happen to the ungodly." (2 Pet. 2:5-6)*

But did God completely abandon His purpose of establishing His Kingdom government or the rule of His Word on earth after the fall of man?

Key Statements

- God's purposes from the beginning do not change.

- Every major and final biblical truth is stated in the book of Genesis.

- Adam and Eve were created in the image and likeness of God and endowed with power to dominate all of God's creation, operating above the forces of Satan that already existed on earth.

- Man was created by God to govern the earth, but within the confines of God's sovereign and dominating Word.

- God's Kingship means that any form of rebellion against His authority purports disconnection from His provisions.

- Disobedience to God's Word or the rebellion against His Kingdom government is the cause of confusion, war, stress, diseases, and poverty and so called "natural disasters."

- It is evident from the beginning that God will take His property (the earth) from people that are rebellious to His rule.

GOD'S PLAN IN THE OLD TESTAMENT

Most believers do not appreciate the Old Testament be-cause they fail to see its continuity to the New Testament. Behind the captivating life accounts of the patriarchs, prophets, judges, and other very interesting characters was the purpose of God to be unveiled in the New Testament.

- *These are a shadow of the things that were to come; the reality, however, is found in Christ. (Col. 2:17)*

In this chapter, I am going to highlight some of the main events in the Old Testament that portrayed God's purpose for the earth. We will find out the motivation behind the acts of God in His relationship with the people of the earth at the time.

**Please take a few minutes to ponder the
proceeding, prodding questions.**

**Have you ever wondered why God made earth the residence
for man, when He could have let us live in heaven with Him?**
*"Then God said, 'Let us make mankind in our image, in our likeness,
so that they may rule over the fish in the sea and the birds in the sky,
over the livestock and all the wild animals, and over all the creatures
that move along the ground.'" (Gen. 1:26)*

**After the fall of man (see Gen. 3), note that there was no
promise of heaven to man. The only promise God made was
that the seed of the woman would crush the head of the
snake, which will in turn bruise his (i.e., the seed's) heel.
The promise had to do with authority taken back from the
snake (Satan) and given back to man through the seed of the
woman.** *"And I will put enmity between you and the woman, and
between your offspring and hers; he will crush your head, and you
will strike his heel."(Gen. 3:15)*

**Why was Noah, whom God deemed righteous, set apart,
saved, and commanded to reproduce and fill the earth,
spared—while all else that were unrighteous in His generation destroyed by God through the flood?** *"The LORD then
said to Noah, 'Go into the ark, you and your whole family, because
I have found you righteous in this generation.'" (Gen. 7:1)*

**Why did God choose Abraham out of all the people on earth
at the time?** *"For I have chosen him, so that he will direct his*

children and his household after him to keep the way of the LORD by doing what is right and just, so that the LORD will bring about for Abraham what he has promised him." (Gen. 18:19)

Why was Abraham asked by God to move away from his family of idol worshippers in order to enter into a covenant to obey God, so that God in return would expand and make him the father of many nations? *"The LORD had said to Abram, 'Go from your country, your people and your father's household to the land I will show you.'" (Gen. 12:1)*

Why did God zealously protect Abraham? *He even told Abraham that He would bless those who blessed him and curse those who cursed him.* *"I will bless those who bless you, and whoever curses you I will curse; and all peoples on earth will be blessed through you." (Gen. 12:3)*

Why did God destroy Sodom and Gomorrah? *"Then the LORD said, 'The outcry against Sodom and Gomorrah is so great and their sin so grievous.'" (Gen. 18:20)*

Why did God protect and prosper Abraham's line of descendants, Isaac and Jacob? *"After Abraham's death, God blessed his son Isaac, who then lived near Beer Lahai Roi." (Gen. 25:11)*

Why did God allow the rest of Abraham's descendants into slavery in Egypt, so that He could rescue and set them apart to live in obedience to Him? *"Then the LORD said to him, 'Know for certain that for four hundred years your descendants will* *be strangers in a country not their own and that they will be enslaved and mistreated there.'" (Gen. 15:13)*

Why did God threaten to wipe out the Israelites who complained and disobeyed Him, so He could start a new people of His own through Moses? *"Now leave me alone so that my anger may burn against them and that I may destroy them. Then I will make you into a great nation." (Ex. 32:10)*

Why did God let all the disobedient generation of the Israelites die so as to continue His covenant with their children? *"The Israelites had moved about in the wilderness forty years until all the men who were of military age when they left Egypt had died, since they had not obeyed the LORD. For the LORD had sworn to them that they would not see the land he had solemnly promised their ancestors to give us, a land flowing with milk and honey." (Joshua 5:6)*

Why did God often instruct the Israelites to wipe out all the other nations they fought that were idol worshippers? *"Then they burned the whole city and everything in it, but they put the silver and gold and the articles of bronze and iron into the treasury of the LORD's house." (Joshua 6:24)*

Why did God make deals with the Israelites that as long as they would obey Him, He would protect them, keep them healthy, prosper them, and increase their number, but if they disobeyed Him, He would send curses on them to destroy them? *"This day I call the heavens and the earth as witnesses against*

24

you that I have set before you life and death, blessings and curses. Now choose life, so that you and your children may live." (Deut. 30:19)

Considering the many kings of Israel, why did God choose king David for the lineage of the Messiah and his kingdom as a model after God's own Kingdom? *"After removing Saul, he made David their king. God testified concerning him: 'I have found David, son of Jesse, a man after my own heart; he will do everything I want him to do.'" (Acts 13:22)*

God's Agenda

- *Jesus said to them, "My Father is always at his work to this very day, and I too am working." (John 5:17)*

Based on the above listed events, I would argue that the work God has been doing for over 6000 years now—since the fall of man—is to get His Kingdom government (the rule of His word, values, laws, and principles) working on earth through a people He can call His own.

- *…who gave himself for us to redeem us from all wickedness and to purify for himself a people that are his very own, eager to do what is good. (Titus 2:14)*

If you have ever wondered, like I have, why God has tolerated for many centuries the suffering, blasphemy, wickedness, immorality, and inexpressively evil things that are increasing and multiplying today, there is your answer; God is working on a special people for Himself. Everything He does on earth is directed towards producing a people zealous for good works on earth—a people that will belong to Him unreservedly: holy, separated, sanctified, and serving and glorying Him. This is why we were taught by Jesus to petition, *"Let thy Kingdom come and your will be done on earth as it is in heaven (Matt. 6:10)"* in our prayer.

- *"For truly I tell you, until heaven and earth disappear, not the smallest letter, not the least stroke of a pen, will by any means disappear from the Law until everything is accomplished." (Matt 5:18)*

Through the Scriptures, God has revealed three main dwelling places for Himself: the tabernacle of Moses, the temple of Solomon and now God seeks to dwell in the temple of our bodies. God is His Word. He is present wherever His Word is being lived out or obeyed. So God's purpose is for His Word (laws and principles) to be our way of life or culture on earth.

- *What agreement is there between the temple of God and idols? For we are the temple of the living God. As God has said: "I will live with them and walk among them, and I will be their God, and they will be my people." (2 Cor. 6:16)*

Satan's Agenda

This exposes the adversary or Satan's major purpose: to rule out the authority of God's Word on earth. He is doing the exact opposite, perpetually promoting immorality or unrighteousness on earth. It is a battle to gain and hold more ground on earth, expressed in righteousness or unrighteousness, good or evil people occupying the earth. We must understand that Satan has always craved to rule as a king. He had a failed attempt to overthrow God and was expelled from heaven. Satan now seeks to be king on earth and is instituting a kingdom that is solely built on contradiction and disobedience to God's laws and principles.

- …*"in which you used to live when you followed the ways of this world and of the ruler of the kingdom of the air, the spirit who is now at work in those who are disobedient."* (Eph. 2:2)

As long as Adam and Eve obeyed God's command, Satan knew they were under God's Kingdom government authority, therefore he (Satan) had no control over them. He proceeded to trick them to believe that God's presence, with them through His Word, was not good enough. By thriving on their spiritual insufficiency, Satan deceived them to step out of the boundaries of God's Word. Man lost the presence (government) of God and consequently lost access to God's provisions.

Who You Obey Is Your King

When we disobey God's Word, we enhance Satan's kingdom and satisfy his craving to rule as king on earth. For this reason, God's priority and primary interest is not in our worship and sacrifices, but in our lifestyle. Jesus puts it this way;

- *"Therefore, if you are offering your gift at the altar and there remember that your brother or sister has something against you, leave your gift there in front of the altar. First go and be reconciled to them; then come and offer your gift." (Matt 4:23 &24)*

Satan's temptation to Jesus reveals that his most prevalent strategy is to use wealth, fame, and power as tools to get people to reject God's Word, thereby submitting to his (Satan's) kingdom. Satan does not care about what you have or don't have. He only cares how you live—your lifestyle—because that is what activates or deactivates his kingdom government of darkness. Think about the whole experiment with Job in the Bible; his objective wasn't just to get Job sick and poor, but ultimately to get him to curse and abandon God. Satan's only objective in this age is to rule out the authority of God's Word (Kingdom government) on earth through worldly governments, in an effort to expand his reign in the kingdom of darkness. **But does God have His own government in place to expand the Sovereign rule of His word on earth?**

Key Statements

- The work God has been doing, for over 6000 years now since the fall of man, is to get His Kingdom government (the rule of His word, values, laws, and principles) working on earth through a people He can call His own.

- Satan's major purpose to rule out the authority of God's Word on earth. He is doing the exact opposite, perpetually promoting immorality or unrighteousness on earth.

- It is a battle to gain and hold more ground on earth, expressed in righteousness or unrighteousness, good or evil people occupying the earth.

- Satan does not care about what you have or don't have. He only cares how you live—your lifestyle—because that is what activates or deactivates his kingdom government of darkness.

- When we disobey God's Word, we enhance Satan's kingdom and satisfy his craving to rule as king on earth.

- Satan sometimes uses wealth, fame, and power as tools to get people to ignore or operate outside of God's Word, thereby submitting to his (Satan's) kingdom.

- Satan sometimes uses wealth, fame, and power as tools to get people to ignore or operate outside God's Word, thereby submitting to his (Satan's) kingdom.

WHAT OR WHO IS
THE CHURCH?

If there is a God, One that claims to be love and is all-powerful, why does He allow oppression and injustice on earth? Why doesn't He put an end to the confusion, war, poverty, disease and awful lot of devastation that afflicts the human race? Why is He silent? It is not as if He doesn't see what's going on, because it is claimed that He is all-seeing and all-knowing. Could it be that He just doesn't care?

Some atheists do not hesitate to pose such questions to devoted Christians any chance they get. An atheist of course has decided to live by their own standards, by defining life in their own terms, because they don't see any "real" evidence of God. To some of them, if there exists an all-powerful and loving God, there must be at least some evidence of His hand of help in a broken world that is ever searching for solutions. I agree. I believe in a God that is not only good for our praises and worship, but One that would care enough to rescue us from the turmoil in our world.

So Is God in Control of the World?

While natural creation may reflect God's orderly, loving and caring traits, the governing systems of the world do not. We can all testify to the rampant corruption, war, fear, injustice, greed, poverty, diseases, death, etc., in the world. This is because unlike the rest of creation, such as plants, animals, the solar system, and so on, God gave man a free will that permits us the choice between aligning with His government or inventing our own. The sad reality is that the world for the most part, through the fall of Adam and Eve, is operating by our own idea of government.

Since government is the source of order, God could not just watch as men drove His creation to destruction with corrupted systems of government. Through Christ, God intervened in the governing systems of the world with His original Kingdom government. In its simplest form, the Kingdom of God is the righteous power and authority of God to justifiably rule over and protect all His creation, including man. This chapter deals with God's Kingdom government on earth.

Who is Jesus?

The prophet Isaiah prophesied the coming of a Son with "the government" on His shoulders:

- *For to us a child is born, to us a son is given, and the government will be on his shoulders. And he will be called Wonderful Counselor, Mighty God, Everlasting Father, Prince of Peace. (Isa 9:6)*

This, along with many other prophecies, pointed to Jesus, who came not only as a prophet, teacher, healer, etc., but as a fulfillment to the prophecies—the anticipated seed of the woman promised in Genesis, the sent one, and King to restore the lost Kingdom government. All the prophecies concerning the coming of Jesus presented Him as God's appointed Kingdom government leader and king, not as a religious figure. Otherwise there would be no reason for king Herod to be alarmed on hearing about Jesus' birth, to the extent that he ordered all babies under the age of two to be killed (see Matt. 2:16). Yes, the first attack launched at Jesus was not from the religious Pharisees but from a rival king. It would interest you to learn that the gifts presented by the Magi from the East to the baby Jesus confirmed His mission on earth. The myrrh stood for His death, the frankincense stood for His priesthood, but the gold stood for His Kingship. Biblically, the number twelve stands for government. There is no doubt that Jesus was setting up His government when He specifically chose twelve disciples, just as God's government over the nation of Israel was founded on twelve tribes.

- *In the time of those kings, the God of heaven will set up a kingdom that will never be destroyed, nor will it be left to another people. It will crush all those kingdoms and bring them to an end, but it will itself endure forever. (Dan. 2:44)*

Heralding the King
John the Baptist Introduces the King

Kings are associated with heralds. A herald is a person with authority from a king who goes to a particular area concerned and makes a proclamation of the will or decision of the king in that place. John the Baptist was the herald sent by God to make a formal announcement and introduce King Jesus to the people of Israel.

- *In those days John the Baptist came, preaching in the wilderness of Judea and saying, "Repent, for the kingdom of heaven has come near." This is he who was spoken of through the prophet Isaiah: "A voice of one calling in the wilderness, 'Prepare the way for the Lord, make straight paths for him.'"* (Matt. 3:1–3)

The King Introduces His Kingdom

When Jesus appeared on the scene, He declared the arrival of the Kingdom government of Heaven and went about teaching His principles to His followers. These were principles of peace, further confirming Isaiah's prophecy that He was to be known as the Prince of Peace, whose Kingdom would be marked by righteousness, justice, and peace.

An interesting event to note is that before Jesus could make a declaration to build His Church, He first had to be sure His disciples were clear about His identity.

- *"But what about you?" he asked. "Who do you say I am?" (Matt. 16:15). And Simon Peter answered and said, Thou art the Christ, the Son of the living God. (Matt 16:16, KJV)*

It was only after Peter, through revelation, had correctly identified Jesus as "the Christ" (meaning Anointed King) that Jesus could make a declaration to build His Church:

- *And I tell you that you are Peter, and on this rock I will build my church, and the gates of Hades will not overcome it. (Matt 16:18)*

But was Jesus referring to a place of worship, as in a building?

The Meaning of Church

I spent some of my early childhood years with my grandmother. In a village that mostly comprises of mud houses, the brick-built, palatial Roman church building was the center of attraction, and that was not just because it was perceived as a residence for the presence of God. For a good many years, the huge, well-decorated Catholic buildings firmly impressed on my mind popped whenever I heard the word "church." My perception of the church as a building that houses the presence of God fueled hypocrisy, as I saved my best behavior for only church services. The dictionary, as it has done for some Scriptural words, incorrectly defines the Church as a place where Christians worship. But the word "Church" translates the original Greek word "ekklesia" which means "called-out" or chosen ones. It has to do with a people that are chosen to represent a government; in this case, the Kingdom government of God on earth. "Church" in the context of the New Testament has nothing to do with a building or a place of worship. Understanding this opens you up to God's purpose and gives you a whole new perspective of the role of the Church in our contemporary society.

The Church Is a People, Not a Building

- *They replied, "It has taken forty-six years to build this temple, and you are going to raise it in three days?" But the temple he had spoken of was his body. (John 2:20–21)*

Jesus, in His conversation with the Pharisees, made a reference to a temple (a place of worship) to mean His own body. He also went ahead and said the following to the Samaritan woman at the well who asked Him about a place of worship:

- *Yet a time is coming and has now come when the true worshipers will worship the Father in the Spirit and in truth, for they are the kind of worshipers the Father seeks. God is spirit, and his worshipers must worship in the Spirit and in truth." (John 4:23–24)*

We can conclude from the Scriptures that the era where temples or specific buildings were set aside as "holy," because they were used in worship to God, ended with Jesus. The human body is now God's chosen temple. Paul the Apostle, by revelation, correctly defines the Church in the following scriptures:

- *For just as each of us has one body with many members, and these members do not all have the same function, so in Christ we, though many, form one body, and each member belongs to all the others. (Rom. 12:4–5)*

- *For the husband is the head of the wife as Christ is the head of the church, his body, of which he is the Savior. (Eph. 5:23)*

The Church Represents God's Kingdom Government on Earth

The Church is a gathering or assembly of people who pledge their allegiance to Christ as their Lord and King. Together they form the "body of Christ." Why is this simple, scriptural-based definition important? Because in Isaiah's prophesy, the government of the earth was to be on the shoulders of the Son (Christ). Now my question to you is, where are our shoulders located? That's right, the shoulders are on the body.

If Jesus (the Son, head) brought a government (Kingdom of Heaven) on His shoulders, and the Church is His body, then the Church (assembly of believers) is the agency for His authority and government on earth. The head administrates authority through the body. The Church therefore is the avenue for the physical expression of the political structure of God's Kingdom government on earth. It is not accidental that Jesus promised to give His Church keys (principles or laws) that will control all the affairs of the earth.

- *I will give you the keys of the kingdom of heaven; whatever you bind on earth will be bound in heaven, and whatever you loose on earth will be loosed in heaven." (Matt 16:19)*

The Church is the final product and motivation behind all the acts of God in the Old Testament, most of which I listed in Chapter 3. Please permit me to recap some important points from the previous chapter.

Man's act of disobedience in the garden was also an act of rebellion against God's Kingdom government. But we know that God did not completely give up on us, because He made a promise that a seed of the woman would be born that would restore His Kingdom government on earth. This promise was in reference to Jesus, who came to institute the Kingdom government of Heaven on earth through His Church.

Government Terminology in the Bible

It will interest you to know that most words in the Bible, especially in the New Testament, connoted as religious, are actually political government terminology. Let's go through a few examples:

- "To repent" means to reform.

- "Messiah" means Government leader (King) who was to be the deliverer of the Israelites and non-Israelites from oppression.

- "Elect" is the same word that is used in worldly governments, which means "appoint." The only difference is that in worldly governments, other men make the appointments, whereas in God's Kingdom government, He appoints.

- "Anointing" is the authority for Kingship, not in a religious sense but in a government context. David, Saul, and many other kings of Israel were anointed.

- "Sin" literally means offense or crime.

- "Ambassadors" are representatives of another country. The Bible refers to believers as ambassadors on earth.

- "Heaven" is the rule or seat of the government of God.

- "Righteousness" means to be in right standing with God's government authority.

- Words such as "condemned" and "justified" are all government legal terms.

Let's look at more examples. Instead of priest in a Jewish context, the New Testament uses the word "apostle," which is of Roman origin. Apostle was a word used to describe an official of the Roman kingdom government who was sent into a nation that had been conquered by Rome—to set up a community with the aim of transforming their culture to Roman culture.

The word "evangelist" is also of Roman government origin; the Romans did not have radios and televisions to broadcast the news of their victory when they conquered a new territory, so there were people specifically appointed to go from town to town announcing the "good news" of victory or "the gospel" as it is better known by believers.

As you can see, Jesus did not even pattern the New Testament covenant after the principles of the Jewish religion, because He didn't come to start or reform the Jewish religion. He came as a government leader, a King. Therefore, most of the terminology of the New Testament is patterned after the Roman kingdom government of the day.

What about the Bible? It is God's constitution on how His Kingdom government operates. It contains laws, promises, principles, rights, and privileges for citizens of His Kingdom government. As I have pointed out, most of the words used in it are governmental, and not religious.

It will interest you to know that the ancient kingdom of Rome under the emperor Constantine was once thought of as the kingdom of God on earth. We know it was not because it collapsed. According to the Prophet Isaiah, God's Kingdom government on earth will have no end. The true Church that operates on the laws and principles of God, as taught by Jesus, is God's Kingdom government on earth, not some man-made institutions.

The Judiciary Component of a Government

A judiciary system is a very significant component of every government, including the Kingdom government of God. As a matter of fact, you cannot separate government from a judiciary system because successful enforcement of laws demands violators of the laws to be judged. Do you now see why words like "judgment" are all through the Bible? There are many references in the Bible to God as The Judge. Most of us are very familiar with the truth that God is forgiving. But are you aware that there can only be forgiveness where there is judgment? We received forgiveness from God through Christ because we were judged as guilty. Jesus is not only God's appointed savior of mankind, but also a King and Judge.

- *He commanded us to preach to the people and to testify that he is the one whom God appointed as judge of the living and the dead. All the prophets testify about him that everyone who believes in him receives forgiveness of sins through his name. (Acts 10:42–43)*

If the Church is indeed God's Kingdom government on earth, then we must also be assigned the judiciary aspect of governmental responsibility. Well, let's look at the scripture below,

- *If any of you has a dispute with another, do you dare to take it before the ungodly for judgment instead of before the Lord's people? Or do you not know that the Lord's people will judge the world? And if you are to judge the world, are you not competent to judge trivial cases? Do you not know that we will judge angels? How much more the things of this life! Therefore, if you have disputes about such matters, do you ask for a ruling from those whose way of life is scorned in the church? I say this to shame you. Is it possible that there is nobody among you wise enough to judge a dispute between believers? But instead, one brother takes another to court—and this in front of unbelievers! (1 Cor. 6:1–6)*

The Internal and External Expression of the Kingdom

- • *And when he was demanded of the Pharisees, when the kingdom of God should come, he answered them and said,*

The kingdom of God cometh not with observation: Neither shall they say, Lo here! or, lo there! For, behold, the kingdom of God is within you. (Luke 17:20–21, KJV)

This statement made by Jesus would have confounded the Pharisees of His day as it does many believers of today. Contrary to the idea of a Kingdom government as being only a visible external organization, Jesus stated to the Pharisees that His Kingdom first rules in the heart of man. It first changes our very nature. All other invented forms of government by men, whether democracy, socialism, communism, or even man's own version of kingdom governments, are merely external organizational institutions. This is why they all fail. The problem is not so much the system or structure of government as it is the corrupted and sinful nature of humankind. The Kingdom government of God therefore first changes the hearts of man and then expresses itself externally in a society of a redeemed people we refer to as the church.

A "New Creation" Government

There is no kingdom without a king because a king is the embodiment of His kingdom. In the Kingdom of God, repentance and submission to Christ (salvation) is the first requirement. This act dethrones "self-will" and enthrones King Jesus in your heart. Our inherited rebellious nature from our first parents (Adam and Eve) is dislodged at this stage, hence we are empowered and predisposed to live by the will of God. This great lesson can be picked up from the exodus of Israel: that when a people are delivered from the bondage of slavery without change of heart, they return to the old way of thinking and acting and eventually back to the bondage of slavery. The superiority of the Kingdom of God over all forms of worldly governments is highlighted in its ability to engage the heart of man and deal with the sinful nature.

- *I will give them an undivided heart and put a new spirit in them; I will remove from them their heart of stone and give them a heart of flesh. Then they will follow my decrees and be careful to keep my laws. They will be my people, and I will be their God. (Eze. 11: 19-20)*

- *Therefore, if anyone is in Christ, the new creation has come: The old has gone, the new is here! (1 Cor. 5:17)*

Differences in the Laws of Moses and Kingdom Laws Taught by Jesus

What makes a government is the making, execution and enforcement of laws. The laws of the Kingdom government of heaven are essentially different from the laws of Moses. The children of Israel were ruled by the external laws of God but in the Kingdom of God, these laws rule in the hearts of believers. For example, in the Law of Moses, the *act* of murder and adultery is against the law. In the Kingdom government of Heaven, the *feeling* of prolonged anger and lust is against the law. (see Matt. 5). This is why Jesus said:

- *For I say unto you, that except your righteousness shall exceed the righteousness of the scribes and Pharisees, ye shall in no case enter into the kingdom of heaven. (Matt. 5:20, KJV)*

The reason for the difference is that the laws of the Kingdom government of Heaven are designed for spirit-regenerated (born-again) people. The act of sin is first a spiritual experience that occurs in the heart before it manifests. Since the Kingdom of God is sensitive to our spirits (hearts), sin is defined at that level. For example, the act of adultery begins in the heart in the form of lust. Jesus, referring to the contradiction in the evil harbored in the heart as opposed to the hypocritical righteous acts, accused the Pharisees of cleaning the outside of the cup but leaving the inside unclean.

Difference Between the Kingdom of God and the Kingdom of Heaven

The Kingdom of God

Jesus, teaching on submission to the Kingdom of God, made reference to the lilies of the field and the birds of the air. This implies that the reign of the Kingdom of God is present in creatures such as plants and animals. This is because they have no *free will* to decide otherwise. The Kingdom of God is also present in humans who by an act of *will* have submitted to the Lordship of Jesus in their heart. When a person becomes born again, the Kingdom of

God comes within them. The Kingdom of God is simply the authority of God expressed in the lifestyle of an individual through obedience to His laws and principles. The internal world (heart) of man is conquered by God.

The Kingdom of Heaven

The gospel of Matthew focuses on the Messiahship of Jesus. He uses the phrase "the Kingdom of Heaven" to emphasize the political structure and government of the country of Heaven. The Kingdom of Heaven has more to do with the collective "heavenly" lifestyle of God's Kingdom citizens. The Kingdom of Heaven on earth is the society of redeemed people or a colony of heaven on earth living by the laws and principles of God. It is when believers collectively model Heaven on earth. It is simply what the true church of God should be. A community or nation of born-again believers living by the laws and principles of God can be rightfully described as the Kingdom of Heaven on earth. The external world of man is subjugated by God.

New Place, New Rules

I was born and raised in Ghana. When I migrated to Australia, I was met with a completely different culture. The laws were different, hence people behaved differently. Even though I migrated from an English-speaking country, I still found it difficult to understand the Australian accent. Like most Western countries, they were very time-conscious. Their educational, economic and healthcare system was different to everything that I had known in Ghana. The day I landed on the Australian soil, I had the responsibility to obey their laws, though I was used to a certain way of living in Africa. I had to *"renew my mind"* and adjust my actions to suit my new country. There were two requirements for me to be accepted as a member of the community of Australians and to be eligible for its benefits:

- Firstly, I had to be a citizen.

- Secondly, I had to be a *responsible* citizen, which involves complying with the laws of the Australian government.

Similarly, the Kingdom of Heaven is a country with different laws, culture, and both economic and healthcare systems, and so on. There are two main requirements to be accepted as member of the community of Heaven.

- Firstly, you have to be a citizen (Born-again)

- Secondly, you have to be a *responsible* citizen. This means renewing your mind in order to comply with the demands of your new country or environment, to successfully live as a member of the community of Heaven (believers on earth). We will look at this in more detail in chapter 11.

So is the Kingdom of God coming, or is it already here?

- *Jesus replied, "Very truly I tell you, no one can **see** the kingdom of God unless they are born again." (John 3:3)*

- *Jesus answered, "Very truly I tell you, no one can **enter** the kingdom of God unless they are born of water and the Spirit. (John 3:5)*

We all have dreams or visions of things we want to do, places we want to be, how we want to live, etc. But they will continue to remain as visions until we take the necessary steps to make them a reality. We may be "seeing" or discerning those things but we have not yet "entered" or attained them.

Likewise, when we repent and submit to Jesus, God makes His home in us and the Kingdom of God comes within us. We begin to "*see*" or discern the Kingdom of God. But we only "*enter*" or attain the Kingdom by connecting and sharing our lives with the community or family of believers who are cooperatively modelling the culture of Heaven on earth by obedience to the King. God made His home in us when we got saved, but we make our home in God when we connect our lives with the family of believers.

- *If anyone acknowledges that Jesus is the Son of God, God lives in them and they in God. (1 John 4:15)*

The Kingdom government of God is therefore not limited to a spiritual experience, but it also means a social transformation and orientation of the Church. Yes, it is here now in our hearts spiritually but we must attain it socially.

Representing the God's Kingdom Government

It is the responsibility of the Church in any place to model the Kingdom of Heaven by our attitude and our relationship with each other. We must challenge the world with a glimpse of the Kingdom government of Heaven. People in the world should be able to look at us and see the reign of the Kingdom of God in our individual lives; they must also be able to look at the community of believers and see the expression of the Kingdom of Heaven in righteousness, peace, and joy in the Holy Spirit. If the world does not see this, they will not listen to our message. This is why Jesus said, the message of the Kingdom must be preached not just in word but as a witness. In other words the world must be able to "see" what we are preaching (see. Matt 24:14). The objective of the Church then, is to convert and establish the Kingdom of God in the hearts of people trapped under the worldly governing systems, so that the governing system of the Kingdom government of Heaven can take a full expression here on earth.

How God's Kingdom Government Functions

- *When the righteous thrive, the people rejoice; when the wicked rule, the people groan. (Prov. 29:2)*

The Church is the body of Christ. Christ is in control of the earth when His body (the Church) takes over the government of the earth (see Eph. 1:23). In the first chapter, I explained that wherever there are people, laws and a leader, there is some form of government.

- God's kingdom government is present wherever any two or three meet acknowledging Jesus as King (Matt. 18:20). The King is the embodiment of His Kingdom.

- Our constitution (laws, principles, rights, privileges) is sourced from the Bible. (Matt. 4:4)

- The Holy Spirit is the governor. He teaches and helps us to learn the ways of the Kingdom of Heaven. (John 16:13)

- God supplies our needs through member support for each other (kingdom commonwealth). (Acts 2:25)

- Healthcare provision is through healing by faith. (James 5:14)

- Defence for citizens is through God's spiritual army (angels). (Matt. 26:53)

As you can see, God has equipped every church regardless of denomination or number to operate independently of worldly governments. The only requirement is to renew our minds in order to adopt the system of God's Kingdom government of Heaven on earth.

Operational Structure of God's Kingdom on Earth

Below is the operational structure of the Kingdom government of God. Jesus is the head, and then apostles, prophets, evangelists, pastors and teachers have a responsibility to train and perfect the body (the Church) to live as a society of Heaven on earth. The Church also has a responsibility deliver the people of the world from their corrupted governments into the Kingdom government of Heaven represented by Church. Let me note here that, in the Kingdom government of God, the leaders are to serve not to be served. The greatest is the servant of all, as Jesus Himself demonstrated.

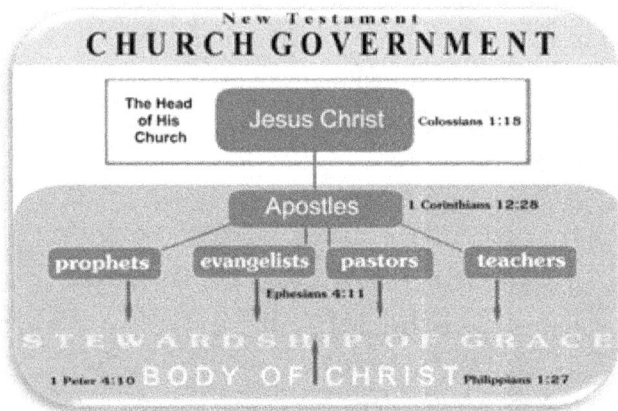

New Testament
CHURCH GOVERNMENT

The Head of His Church | Jesus Christ | Colossians 1:18

Apostles — 1 Corinthians 12:28

prophets | evangelists | pastors | teachers

Ephesians 4:11

STEWARDSHIP OF GRACE

1 Peter 4:10 BODY OF CHRIST Philippians 1:27

source: www.s8wministries.org

Persecution of the Church

The biggest threat to worldly governing systems is the existence of communities that operate independently of theirs. Governments do not hesitate to break up small independent communities, hence the persecution of the early church. The Church may begin to experience increased persecution from worldly governments when we start to effectively operate as an independent Kingdom government of God. But that's nothing new. Since its conception, the church has been marked by persecution. It is the one thing that is promised in the life of every true believer. It was said about the early church that as it began to slowly accept the paganistic ways of ancient Rome, the persecution reduced. The authenticity of a church can be measured by the level of persecution she faces from "pagan" worldly governments.

- *In fact, everyone who wants to live a godly life in Christ Jesus will be persecuted. (2 Tim. 3:12)*

What about So-called Christian Nations?

We should not be deceived by nations such as America that claim to have chosen God and therefore belong to God. As far as God is concerned, He does the choosing; no one chooses God. God is a King, and unlike other forms of government, Kings elect their citizens, not the other way around.

- *But the plans of the LORD stand firm forever, the purposes of his heart through all generations. Blessed is the nation whose God is the LORD, the people he chose for his inheritance. (Psalm 33:11–12)*

- *You did not choose me, but I chose you and appointed you so that you might go and bear fruit—fruit that will last—and so that whatever you ask in my name the Father will give you. (John 15:16)*

- *But you are a chosen people, a royal priesthood, a holy nation, God's special possession, that you may declare the praises of him who called you out of darkness into his wonderful light. (1 Pet. 2:9)*

There is no pattern anywhere in the Bible of God entering into a permanent relationship with a person, group, or nation except on the basis of a covenant. God chose Israel by a covenant with Abraham and subsequently chose the church through the blood covenant of Christ as agency for His government on earth. Every other nation or people is governed by rulers of darkness. The world apart from the Church is simply fallen men governed by fallen systems of government.

What about Romans 13?

I know at this stage, if you are thorough in the Scriptures, you are probably questioning how Romans 13 applies, which implies to submit to all governing authorities because they are all ordained by God.

I believe the misinterpretation of this chapter in the book of Romans is the reason why the body of Christ (the Church) has perhaps willingly or unwillingly participated in or supported worldly governments that continue to pass laws against God's Word, thereby destabilizing our societies.

Below is the passage of scripture in full context.

Romans 13:

1Let everyone be subject to the governing authorities, for there is no authority except that which God has established. The authorities that exist have been established by God. *2Consequently, whoever rebels against the authority is rebelling against what God has instituted, and those who do so will bring judgment on themselves. 3For rulers hold no terror for those who do right, but for those who do wrong. Do you want to be free from fear of the one in authority? Then do what is right and you will be commended. 4For the one in authority is God's servant for your good. But if you do wrong, be afraid, for rulers do not bear the sword for no reason. They are God's servants, agents of wrath to bring punishment on the wrongdoer. 5Therefore, it is necessary to submit to the authorities, not only because of possible punishment but also as a matter of conscience. 6This is also why you pay taxes, for the authorities are God's servants, who give their full time to governing. 7Give to everyone what you owe them: If you owe taxes, pay taxes; if revenue, then revenue; if respect, then respect; if honor, then honor. 8Let no debt remain outstanding, except the continuing debt to love one another, for whoever loves others has fulfilled the law. 9The commandments, "You shall not commit adultery," "You shall not murder," "You shall not steal," "You shall not covet," and whatever other command there may be, are summed up in this one command: "Love your neighbor as yourself." 10Love does no harm to a neighbor. Therefore love is the fulfillment of the law.*

Please note carefully that the above passage is in reference to, and only applicable to a righteous government. As we read from verse 9, the government authorities are established by God to enforce the moral codes and ordinances of God, which are:

- The commandments, *"You shall not commit adultery," "You shall not murder," "You shall not steal," "You shall not covet," and whatever other command there may be, are summed up in this one command: "Love your neighbor as yourself." Love does no harm to a neighbor. Therefore, love is the fulfillment of the law.*

Any form of government that violates these foundational moral codes of God is not of God, and therefore we are not obliged to submit to that government. It is Satan who works in the sons of disobedience to God's Word (see Eph. 2:2). God warned ancient Israel that they are not even to heed to prophets who were able to prophesy signs and wonders that came to pass, if their intention was to lead them away from God (see Deut. 13:1–4). As far as God is concerned, whoever is not for Him is against Him (see Matt. 12:30).

Does God Contradict Himself?

Note what it says in verse 4 of Romans 13: *"For the one in authority is God's servant for your good. But if you do wrong, be afraid, for rulers do not bear the sword for no reason. They are God's servants, agents of wrath to bring punishment on the wrongdoer."*

To be a servant of God is to be under His commands. If we say that God ordains evil governments that pass laws against His Word, then what we are really saying is that God contradicts His Word. Jesus said, *"Every kingdom divided against itself will not stand.."* (see Matt. 12:25). How can God establish a government that opposes His Word and purpose for the earth—when all

He has done, is doing, and wants to do is to extend His rule or Kingdom government on earth?

"Your kingdom come, your will be done, on earth as it is in heaven." (Matt. 6:10)

For truly I tell you, until heaven and earth disappear, not the smallest letter, not the least stroke of a pen, will by any means disappear from the Law until everything is accomplished. (Matt. 5:18)

Obey God or Man

When the Pharisees made a law for no one to preach in the name of Jesus, the apostle Peter protested against it and proceeded to act against that law, causing his arrest. Peter would have come across as rebellious by the government authorities of the day. But it was clear that the authorities were not representing God's government, because God proved Peter's innocence when He sent angels to release him from prison. The apostles and the early church would not have been persecuted and martyred if they compromised with the laws of the Roman government. Their loyalty to Christ as their King and their unwillingness to submit to the corrupt Roman government caused their martyrdom.

Are Worldly Governments Really Representing God?

Let's look at consequences of some laws that have been passed against God's Word by worldly governments.

- Approximately 50,000,000 babies are aborted (murdered) across the world every year. Not to mention the many casualities of war because of the adoption of human military as a defence force in worldly governments. God's Word clearly commands against murder in any form and commands us to love even our enemies. (see Exo. 20:13), (see Matt. 5:44).

- Human extinction is being enhanced on earth because same-sex marriage is now being legalized and recognized by governments in many countries. God's clearly warns against homosexuality. (see Levi. 18:22), (see 1 Cor. 6:9– 11)

- The capitalist economic system in democratic societies accounts for the rampant poverty, sickness and death that is prevalent in the world. God's Word instructs us to commit to sharing what we have with those in need. As a matter of fact, God's own is a Kingdom commonwealth economic system that is designed to eliminate poverty. (see Deut. 15:4) (see 2 Cor. 8:14)

Share of world's private consumption, 2005

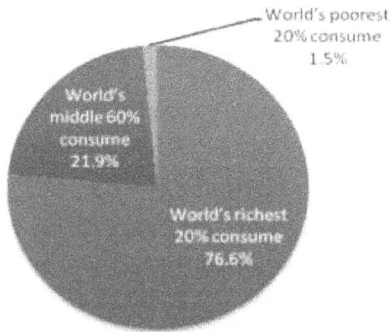

World's poorest 20% consume 1.5%

World's middle 60% consume 21.9%

World's richest 20% consume 76.6%

Source: World Bank Development Indicators 2008

The Need for a righteous Government

As you can see, there is a deliberate attempt by these worldly governments to rule out the authority of God's Word/government and enhance Satan's kingdom on earth. All of the problems we are faced with are the result of evil, corrupt government, and the solution is a righteous government that Jesus has already instituted through His Church.

For those of us who still think worldly governments are representing God's government, here is what the prophet Isaiah, by inspiration of the Holy Spirit, has to say about it.

- *Woe to those who call evil good and good evil, who put darkness for light and light for darkness, who put bitter for sweet and sweet for bitter. (Is. 5:20)*

God has made Jesus king, and any body that is not submitted to Him is a rebel as far as God is concerned. It doesn't even matter if they are good people or not. As Jesus puts it, only God is good. While worldly governments may appear religious, intellectual, and to some extent moral, like the Pharisees in Jesus' day, God has rejected the world and all the society that has not submitted to the righteous government of His appointed King, Jesus.

- *The world and its desires pass away, but whoever does the will of God lives forever. (1 John 2:17)*

Moral corruption is irreversible

Once a fruit, such as an apple, has a small rot in it, no matter how good it may look overall, in time that corruption will infect the whole fruit. We may be able to delay the spread of the rot by refrigerating it, but the decay will eventually run its course through the whole fruit. This is how it is with human nature. Due to the fall of man, the sting of sin continues to linger in mankind, no matter how good they may claim to be. They can postpone that nature from revealing itself, but they cannot prevent it. A test of pressure and time always exposes the true nature of man. This partly explains why we have often been disappointed by people we thought we could trust, whether they are family, friends, or even worldly government officials. Peter the disciple, before he was filled with the Holy Spirit, seemed loyal and faithful to Jesus until he denied Him three times; the rich young ruler who claimed to have obeyed all the laws of God walked away from Jesus when he was told to sell his possessions and give to the poor. There is no other remedy for the corrupted Adamic nature. God's only solution is execution of the old nature and a replacement with new a nature through Christ.

- *Therefore, if anyone is in Christ, the new creation has come: The old has gone, the new is here! (2 Cor. 5:17)*

No Peace Apart from Righteousness

Paul the apostle defined the Kingdom of God as righteousness, peace, and joy in the Holy Spirit. The Holy Spirit defines the boundaries of God's Kingdom government. Where leaders are appointed by majority votes of people and not by the leadership of the Holy Spirit—where there is no expression of righteousness, peace, and joy resulting from a government—the Kingdom government of God is absent. The great deal of talks about peace in our world can never be attained without righteousness. The pursuit for peace bypassing righteousness is an illusion, and only the Kingdom government of God equips men with righteousness through a spiritual birth for rulership.

- *"There is no peace," says the LORD, "for the wicked." (Is. 48:22)*

Incorporated Churches

For tax-exempt purposes and other "legal" accountabilities, most churches register with the state government. This act of incorporation by churches is simply a blend of Christ's kingdom with worldly governments. The Church represents a spiritual entity and must not have any ties with the state constitution or laws. Any such relationship changes its status into a legal entity accountable to the state government. Churches that register with worldly governments submit to all the corporate state laws, which may vary from time to time, especially in democratic governments.

Sovereignty is exclusive. Jesus said, *"No man can serve two masters…" (Matt. 6:24).* Churches that submit to the authority of the state remove Jesus as the Sovereign authority.

- *What harmony is there between Christ and Belial? Or what does a believer have in common with an unbeliever? What agreement is there between the temple of God and idols? For we are the temple of the living God. As God has said: "I will live with them and walk among them, and I will be their God, and they will be my people." Therefore, "Come out from them and be separate, says the Lord. Touch no unclean thing, and I will receive you." And, "I will be a Father to you, and you will be my sons and daughters, says the Lord Almighty." (2 Cor. 6:15–18)*

Unfortunately, most churches knowingly or unknowingly have entered the realm of Caesar, mostly for tax-exempt purposes.

Such churches may claim to be under the Lordship of Christ, but in actual fact, they are state owned and authorized churches.

- *"Tell us then, what is your opinion? Is it right to pay the imperial tax to Caesar or not?" But Jesus, knowing their evil intent, said, "You hypocrites, why are you trying to trap me? Show me the coin used for paying the tax." They brought him a denarius, and he asked them, "Whose image is this? And whose inscription?" "Caesar's," they replied. Then he said to them, "So give back to Caesar what is Caesar's, and to God what is God's." (Matt. 22:17–21)*

While we seek the feeble hand of the government to support God's church through tax-exemptions, instead of trusting God, we replace the sovereign will of God with the sovereign will of the state from which it is ruled.

The Carnal Church

The Church personifies a spiritual entity, the kingdom government of Heaven. A carnal church is one that has lost sight of its eternal nature and source. Such churches function as if there is nothing beyond this life. Their doctrine is heavily influenced by the "cares of life" as Jesus puts it. Most of them focus on prosperity, which really is not the gospel that is to be preached but only a principle to be taught. Due to this, the majority of professing believers have lost their view of eternity and therefore the joy of the Lord.

- *If only for this life we have hope in Christ, we are of all people most to be pitied. (1 Cor. 15:19)*

If we, the Church, claim to belong to Christ but all we are looking for are things in this life (material possessions), then Paul the Apostle says we are the most miserable and pitiful of all people. We may not have committed an obvious sin, but we miss the whole ultimate eternal purpose as God's redeemed people.

The Story of Awesome Jnr. – The Predicament of the Church

There is a story told of a great, loving, wealthy, knowledgeable, wise, understanding, and powerful King. There's nothing you can think of that He lacked. He had an innumerable array of servants who worshipped and served him. He was absolutely awesome, hence his name: The Great King Awesome.

The Great King Awesome had a child whose name was Awesome Jnr. Awesome Jnr. was just like his father, loving, knowledgeable, wise, understanding, and powerful. He was so dearly loved and treasured by his father.

Years passed, and Awesome Jnr. had matured to a responsible age, so The Great King Awesome had an idea. He decided to allow his loved and cherished child, who was now mature, to experience a life of his own away from him but not completely cut off from him. The Great King Awesome, whose wealth was immeasurable, gave Awesome Jnr. one of his territories and sent him on his way to live there. Awesome Jnr. lived like his father. He was the king and dominated everything in his territory. He had a slave at his command.

One day, something terrible happened. Awesome Jnr. tripped and fell, knocking his head. He could no longer remember who he was. He suffered a serious identity crisis. He completely forgot his all-powerful father. He even forgot he had a slave at his command.

Pretty soon Awesome Jnr.'s slave realized that his master had forgotten who he was, so he took advantage of it right away and started ordering Awesome Jnr. around. The master had now become the slave, and the slave the master. Awesome Jnr.'s slave used and abused Awesome Jnr., The slave even went as far as making Awesome Jnr., who had forgotten who he was, worship him.

One day The Great King Awesome sent Awesome Snr., who was Awesome Jnr.'s senior brother, to check on how Awesome Jnr. was doing. Upon his arrival, Awesome Snr. was stunned at what he encountered. Awesome Jnr. was living miserably in his own territory. He did not in any way demonstrate the traits His father. Nothing showed that he was the son of the Great King; what was worse, he was taking orders from his slave while his slave lived like a king and master of the house.

At this, Awesome Snr. was fumed. He rebuked the slave and got him back to his tasks. He then proceeded to remind Awesome

Jnr. that they are brothers and sons of the loving, wealthy, knowledgeable, wise, understanding, and powerful King Awesome. While there, Awesome Snr. made sure that Awesome Jnr. was functioning like the son of a king that he was, taking charge of his own territory.

The time came for Awesome Snr. to leave, and he left in confidence that Awesome Jnr.'s identity crisis was resolved and would function accordingly.

On the contrary, Awesome Jnr., though he had been thoroughly taught about his identity, still didn't have the confidence to function in it. He had gotten comfortable with the life of a slave after the accident. He still saw his slave as his master, and therefore taking control in his territory just didn't seem like something he could do in the absence of his senior brother.

As sad as it sounds, Awesome Jnr. refused to stand his ground against his slave, who craved to dominate him. Awesome Jnr. continued to remain a slave to his slave after his senior brother left. Every now and then Awesome Jnr. would try to believe what his senior brother came to tell him and act upon it, but the slave, realizing the lack of confidence in Awesome Jnr., would overpower him and send him away to continue on as a slave.

- In this story God is depicted as The Great king Awesome

- Jesus is depicted as Awesome Senior

- The Children of God (The Church) is depicted as Awesome Jnr.

- Satan is the slave.

My fellow believers, the corruption, greed, violence, war poverty, diseases etc., will continue on our planet until children of God (the Church) are ready to act boldly on the revelation of who we are, what our Father sent us here to do, and also why Jesus came. The Church, headed by Jesus, is God's appointed and approved rulers on the earth.

Jesus did not only proclaim that the Kingdom of God is "at hand" meaning, "it is here". He demonstrated it by healing the sick, feeding the hungry, casting out demons and discipling people into *the way* of life in the Kingdom of Heaven. By this, Jesus showed that the Kingdom government of Heaven can meet all our needs independent of worldly governments. The true church operating as a Kingdom government under God on earth is a church that imitates Jesus' acts of compassion for the poor and disadvantaged, sets people free spiritually, emotionally and physically, and disciple them into the way of life in the Kingdom.

Key Statements to note

- Natural creation may reflect God's orderly trait, but the governing systems of the world do not.

- Through Christ, God intervened in the governing systems of the world with His original Kingdom government.

- The Kingdom of God is the righteous power and authority of God to justifiably rule over and protect all His creation, including man.

- All the prophecies concerning the coming of Jesus presented Him as God's appointed Kingdom government leader and not a religious figure.

- Jesus was setting up His government when He specifically chose twelve disciples, just as God's government over the nation of Israel was founded on twelve tribes.

- "Church" translates the original Greek word "ekklesia," which means "called-out ones" or chosen ones.

- The era where temples or specific buildings were set aside as "holy" because they were used in worship ended with Jesus.

- The Church is a gathering or assembly of people who pledge their allegiance to Christ as their Lord and King. Together they form the "body of Christ."

- The Church is the final product of the motivation behind all the acts of God in the Old Testament.

- Most words in the Bible, especially in the New Testament, connoted as religious are actually political government terminology.

- There is no Kingdom without a king. A king is the embodiment of His kingdom.

- God has equipped every church, regardless of denomination or number, to operate independently of the world's systems.

- God ordains governments to uphold His moral codes. Any government that violates these moral codes of God is not of God, and therefore, we are not obliged to submit to that government.

5

THE HOLY SPIRIT:
THE GOVERNOR

All Kingdoms Expand by Colonization
Through Governors

Heaven is an actual place. It is a spiritual country under the rule of the Kingdom government of God. All kingdoms expand and have governors responsible for cultivating the culture of the colonizing Kingdom (Heaven) in the people of the new distant colony (earth). In the Kingdom of God, the Holy Spirit is the governor. He leads people to the King, confirms their citizenship, and teaches them the lifestyle of the Kingdom of Heaven. These acts of the Holy Spirit give rise to two groups of people in our world: the children of God, who are under the kingdom government of

God through the indwelling of the Spirit of God, and those of the Kingdom of darkness, who are without the Holy Spirit.

The Importance of the Holy Spirit

Far too little attention has been given to the Holy Spirit, although He is God's personal representative on earth. The Holy Spirit is not only a person but also a place: *"For in him we live and move and have our being. As some of your own poets have said, 'We are his offspring.'" (Acts 17:28)*. He defines the limits of the Kingdom of Heaven. The truth about Jesus as a Savior is stated in only one gospel; however, the introduction to each of the four gospels specifically identifies Jesus as the One who baptizes with the Holy Spirit.

- *I baptize you with water for repentance. But after me comes one who is more powerful than I, whose sandals I am not worthy to carry. He will baptize you with the Holy Spirit and fire. (Matt. 3:11)*

- *"I baptize you with water, but he will baptize you with the Holy Spirit." (Mark 1:8)*

- *John answered them all, "I baptize you with water. But one who is more powerful than I will come, the straps of whose sandals I am not worthy to untie. He will baptize you with the Holy Spirit and fire." (Luke 3:16)*

- *And I myself did not know him, but the one who sent me to baptize with water told me, 'The man on whom you see the Spirit come down and remain is the one who will baptize with the Holy Spirit.' (John 1:33)*

Jesus was careful to repeat the promise with which John the Baptist had introduced Him—that He would be the baptizer of the Holy Spirit (see Acts 1:4–5). Almost all commentators on the Bible agree the fulfillment of this promise to be in the day of Pentecost (see Acts 2:1–4).

It is impossible to overemphasize the importance of the Holy Spirit in the life of every believer. The Holy Spirit initiated the birth of the Church. All aspects of the Christian life therefore revolve around the Holy Spirit. God cannot do anything on earth without His Spirit. The success of the revolutionary earthly ministry of Jesus is attributed to the Holy Spirit. It is simply insurmountable to experience the Kingdom of God on earth without the presence of the governor from Heaven.

- *For the kingdom of God is not a matter of eating and drinking, but of righteousness, peace and joy in the Holy Spirit. (Rom. 14:17)*

First Work of the Holy Spirit – Fruits

There are two successive phases of the Holy Spirit's impact on a believer. Firstly, the Holy Spirit births or regenerates the Spirit of the believer. This phenomenon occurs when one repents and receives Christ as Lord. He/she is translated from the kingdom of darkness to the Kingdom of God. The new believer is endowed with the ability to live according to the new culture of the Kingdom of Heaven. This endowment gives rise to what is known as fruits of the Spirit.

- *But the fruit of the Spirit is love, joy, peace, forbearance, kindness, goodness, faithfulness, gentleness and self-control. Against such things there is no law. (Gal. 5:22–23)*

Second Work of the Spirit – Baptism (Gifts)

Then there is baptism of the Holy Spirit, which follows the regeneration of the spirit. This has to do with the gifts of the Spirit. The believer is given dominion over circumstances. By breathing on His disciples after His resurrection, Jesus regenerated their spirits, but the disciples still lacked the courage to face opposition with their revolutionary message. However, at Pentecost, when they were baptized by the Spirit, they were ready to face the world and accomplish their purpose as apostles. So the first act of the Spirit gives the believer the ability to live right. The second act of the Spirit gives the believer power over circumstances.

- *Now to each one the manifestation of the Spirit is given for the common good. To one there is given through the Spirit a message of wisdom, to another a message of knowledge by means of the same Spirit, to another faith by the same Spirit,*

to another gifts of healing by that one Spirit, to another
miraculous powers, to another prophecy, to another distin-
guishing between spirits, to another speaking in different
kinds of tongues, and to still another the interpretation of
tongues. All these are the work of one and the same Spirit,
and he distributes them to each one, just as he determines.
(1 Cor. 12:7–11)

Combination of the Fruits and Baptism (Gifts)

It is the combination of the fruits (character) and baptism (gifts, power) of the Spirit that makes believers the light and salt of the earth as Jesus described. The Holy Spirit gives believers advantages and sets them apart from unbelievers. When the Holy Spirit is quenched, the lifestyle of the believer often becomes no different from an unsaved person. As I previously mentioned, the Holy Spirit makes all the difference in the life of a believer. We must therefore cherish and yield to His leadership.

Man is Recreated Through the Work of the Holy Spirit

Notice that the Holy Spirit restores the two main things man lost after the fall in the Garden of Eden. Adam and Eve lost the image and likeness (character) of God and dominion (power) to rule the earth. Psychologists have concluded that the greatest craving for humanity is the need for power. It is not a coincidence that after

His resurrection, Jesus first breathed a new Spirit into His disciples and then baptized them with the power of the Holy Spirit. Through the work of the Holy Spirit, man is recreated. We receive the image and likeness and dominion that was lost in the fall.

Evidence of the Holy Spirit

It is clear in the Bible that when people were filled with the Holy Spirit, they spoke in tongues or prophesied in every case. When the heart is filled, the overflow takes place through the mouth in speech (see Matt. 12:34). Speaking in tongues usually marks baptism of the Holy Spirit.

The Need for the Leadership of The Holy Spirit on Earth

The Jewish scientist, Albert Einstein, coined a statement that I believe captures the problem of this world. He said, "Level one problems require level two solutions." In other words, you cannot solve a problem at the same level it was caused. The solutions we seek cannot come from men because we are creating the problems in the first place. We need to submit to a higher authority, one who is not affected by our problems. The very reason why we do not let children solve the biggest problems in the family is the very reason why we need to hand the issues of the earth to the Holy Spirit. The minds of all humans are clouded by the problems that surround us. Our thought patterns are affected, and we are incapable of raising our thoughts above the problems. We need help from above. The Holy Spirit is the one with the answers. He is the promise of the Father that brings the environment of Heaven here on earth for our experience.

The church is the only agency on earth that is equipped to operate by the leadership of the Holy Spirit. Earth will only be able to experience heaven if the Holy Spirit gains full control of it through the church. This means the church must operate as an independent Kingdom government completely under the leadership of the Holy Spirit and spread by influence.

THE KING'S PROVISION FOR
HIS CITIZENS (THE CHURCH)

Worldly Governments are
operating under a curse.

I stated before that all worldly governments are operating under Satan's spiritual kingdom of darkness. The result is corrupted systems of government, which manifest in a culture of sin, poverty, and death. Worldly governing systems are self-destructive. The solutions they present to solve problems create further problems. The prince of the spiritual kingdom operating behind the scenes of these worldly governments uses deception as a medium to steal from, kill, and destroy people (see John 10:10). Hence there are obvious contradictions in its approach to resolve problems. For example, their pursuit of peace is through war; their attempt to reduce or eliminate poverty is the adoption of an economic system such as capitalism, which capitalizes on the poor; how about the hypocrisy in providing health insurance for its citizens and yet legalizing abortion, which accounts for the death of approximately 50,000,000 babies per year worldwide? What this says is "we will look after you if only you can make it through birth." So you see, it is evident that the governing systems of the world are under the curse of rebellion dating all the way back to Adam and Eve.

The Church Is Released from the Curse

The great news is that the King of the Kingdom government of Heaven is benevolent. He does not take advantage of His citizens but acts in their best interests. The holy God made a provision in order to continue His covenant with man through the Israelites.

- *In fact, the law requires that nearly everything be cleansed with blood, and without the shedding of blood there is no forgiveness. (Heb. 9:22)*

The blood of animals was regularly used as atonement for sin until the King of the Kingdom of Heaven, Jesus, came to offer Himself as a sin sacrifice. All who accept Him are reinstated into His Kingdom and released from the curse operating in the world. In that one sacrifice, Jesus dealt with the past, present, and future sins of all human beings on earth but only applicable to those who submit to Him. On the cross, the entire curse due to our sins was placed on Jesus, so that the good due to His perfect obedience would become available to those who will receive Him. Through our King's sacrifice, the body of believers (the Church) is translated from a world operating under a curse to a "world of Heaven" filled with abundant blessings.

- *Christ redeemed us from the curse of the law by becoming a curse for us, for it is written: "Cursed is everyone who is hung on a pole." (Gal. 3:13)*

Government is the single most powerful influence on earth. The condition of the world is a reflection of the governing systems. What the earth needs to escape the curse is the "world of Heaven," and only the Church is equipped to operate in that realm. You can see the necessity for the Church to function as an independent government and eventually take over the government of the whole earth.

- *For the creation waits in eager expectation for the children of God to be revealed. (Rom. 8:19)*

What Salvation Involves

Salvation is often limited to just the forgiveness of sins, but God's salvation program for His Kingdom citizens involves a lot more. The following captures some of the blessings available to citizens of the Kingdom of Heaven (the Church)—news that is so good most believers fail to appropriate due to unbelief. Even the prophet Isaiah on "seeing" what is now available for our experience began his prophesy with the statement: *"Who has believed our message and to whom has the arm of the LORD been revealed?" (Is. 53:1).* I call it the great exchange.

Sin Is Exchanged for Righteousness

The disciple John defined sin as the transgression of the law (1 John 3:4). Jesus did not sin but chose to suffer the consequences of sin for those who could not keep the law and those that had never been under the law. Citizens of His Kingdom are justified (acquitted, not guilty, reckoned righteous, made righteous) by His blood. We are brought into right standing with God without any effort on our part.

- *Since we have now been justified by his blood, how much more shall we be saved from God's wrath through him! (Rom. 5:9)*

Furthermore each member of the body of believers (the Church) is endowed with the ability through the Holy Spirit to operate in principles of justice, love, peace, and so on, which are much needed in our present world.

Poverty Is Exchanged for Abundance

In a world that thrives on scarcity mentality, the majority are engulfed in poverty. King Jesus, through His death and resurrection, released His Church from the curse of poverty and empowered us for wealth.

- *Therefore shalt thou serve thine enemies which the LORD shall send against thee, in hunger, and in thirst, and in nakedness, and in want of all things: and he shall put a yoke of iron upon thy neck, until he have destroyed thee. (Deut. 28:47–48, KVJ)*

God's description of poverty in His warning to the Israelites included hunger, thirst, nakedness, and in need of all things. Jesus was hungry, thirsty, naked on the cross, and was even buried in a borrowed tomb. The King of Heaven became poor so we could share in the wealth of His Kingdom.

- *For ye know the grace of our Lord Jesus Christ, that, though he was rich, yet for your sakes he became poor, that ye through his poverty might be rich. (2 Cor. 8:9, KJV)*

Death Is Exchanged for Life

Jesus never sinned; therefore, He didn't deserve to die but He tasted death so His Church could share in the eternal life He provides. There is no need for the fear of death for those in the Kingdom of God.

- *For the wages of sin is death, but the gift of God is eternal life in Christ Jesus our Lord. (Rom. 6:23)*

Shame Is Exchanged for Glory

Most people carry shame in the world. The King of Heaven was made the object of public shame to the whole world so we could share in His glory. There is no need for anyone in His Kingdom to bear shame of any sort. Jesus took away all our shame.

- *For in Scripture it says: "See, I lay a stone in Zion, a chosen and precious cornerstone, and the one who trusts in him will never be put to shame." (1 Pet. 2:6)*

Rejection Is Exchanged for Acceptance

Feelings of rejection are the source of most repulsive behavior in our societies. Jesus was rejected by His own people. He also felt the rejection by God as He cried out on the cross.

- *About three in the afternoon Jesus cried out in a loud voice, "Eli, Eli, lema sabachthani?" (which means "My God, my God, why have you forsaken me?") (Matt. 27:46)*

The curtain split in the temple of Jerusalem after the death of Jesus symbolised that God now accepts anyone who submits Jesus as their King. Citizens of the Kingdom of Heaven on earth, the Church, enjoy acceptance and fellowship with God and with one another.

Sickness Is Exchanged for Health

The world is dominated by the epidemic of chronic and terminal diseases. Health systems are almost helpless as diseases such as cancer and AIDS continue to devour the lives of many. Sickness is a direct result of the curse. Jesus bore the sickness and pain of all humanity. His Kingdom's citizens (the Church) are entitled to divine health and healing by faith.

- *"He himself bore our sins" in his body on the cross, so that we might die to sins and live for righteousness; "by his wounds you have been healed." (1 Pet. 2:24)*

The World Needs the Church

A culture of sin, poverty, death, shame, rejection, sickness, etc., is the expression of a world operating under the curse. This is a world that has not received the blessings of God offered through Christ. A world that is operating independently of God's Kingdom government. A world that cannot save itself. The Church, through Christ, is empowered with the restoration power of God. It is not even enough for the Church to be present on earth. The world is headed for destruction if the Church doesn't operate as an independent Kingdom government and eventually take control of the wheels of the government of the earth, so as to create a culture consistent with the blessings that have been made available to us through the death sacrifice of our King Jesus Christ.

Overemphasized Grace

What is grace?

Nothing paints a clearer picture of the loving nature of our God than His grace. The highest act of God's grace for us is the provision of salvation through Christ. God's grace, however, is constantly at work in our lives before we even come to know Christ. I do not know about you, but I am not sure why God kept me alive when I was entangled and living in perpetual sin. God did not keep me from His sun, the rain, and the oxygen I needed for my survival.

- *But God demonstrates his own love for us in this: While we were still sinners, Christ died for us. (Rom 5:8)*

I do not say that it was good that man fell in the beginning, but without Adam and Eve's act of disobedience, man may not have come to know the extent of God's grace the way we do now. Man was created and is to be sustained by God. Without the provision of God's grace, we will be cut off from our source, and death would be the inevitable consequence. There would be no hope for any man. The all-righteous God is only able to maintain His relationship with man through His grace.

Is there any other way to be right with God outside of His grace?

Job, in his misery and perplexity, posed a question to his friends. He asked, how could man achieve righteousness with God (see Job 25:4)? In the Old Testament, God chose and gave the nation of Israel His laws through which they could achieve righteousness. The failure of many generations proved that man could not keep the laws; and therefore, could not achieve righteousness.

Job's question, however, was finally answered in the life of Jesus, the only man (Jew) to live without ever breaking any of God's laws; and therefore, the first man ever to stand righteous by successfully keeping all of God's laws. Jesus then went on to give His life as an atoning sacrifice for all those under the law (Jews) that could not keep it and for those that had never been under the law (Gentiles).

But what does the grace of God mean for us?

Does God's grace mean we don't have to live right anymore? Does it mean God now tolerates and does not punish sin anymore? We must understand that God's grace is not a substitute for living right or a license to engage in sinful acts.

- *For God did not call us to be impure, but to live a holy life. (1 Thess. 4:7)*

When God told Adam and Eve "...*the day you eat the fruit of the knowledge of good and evil, you will die,*" he meant a spiritual death, which later manifested in a physical death. Consequently, all the descendants of Adam and Eve, including the nation of Israel, lacked the Spirit to keep the laws of God. It is God's Spirit in man that responds to His spiritual laws.

- *We know that the law is spiritual; but I am unspiritual, sold as a slave to sin. (Rom. 7:14)*

Empowerment by the Holy Spirit

Jesus was conceived by the Holy Spirit. He was alive spiritually; therefore, He could respond to and obey all of God's laws. After atoning for our sins, Jesus has given us the power that would make it possible for us to obey God.

- *His divine power has given us everything we need for a godly life through our knowledge of him who called us by his own glory and goodness. (2 Pet. 1:3)*

While we are not obligated to keep all the Law of Moses, we are now required to keep the righteous requirement of the Law. Let's look at what Paul the apostle says.

- *Therefore, there is now no condemnation for those who are in Christ Jesus, because through Christ Jesus the law of the Spirit who gives life has set you free from the law of sin and death. For what the law was powerless to do because it was weakened by the flesh, God did by sending his own Son in order that **the righteous requirement of the law might be fully met in us, who do not live according to the flesh but according to the Spirit**. (Rom. 8:1–4)* The question that comes to mind then is, what is the righteous requirement of the Law?

Love is The Fulfillment of The Law

Jesus said all the other laws and the prophets hang on it; it is simply to love God and love your neighbor as yourself. If you love your neighbor, you won't steal, murder, covet, etc.

- *Love does no harm to a neighbor. Therefore love is the fulfillment of the law. (Rom. 13:10)*

Love has been tagged the royal law and the law of liberty (James 1:25, 2:8). To stress its importance, "love" as a noun, adjective, and a verb occurs 28 times in 22 verses in 1 John 4: 7–21. We are obligated to love because love activates our new spiritual nature. When we stop loving, we become carnal.

- *The goal of this command is love, which comes from a pure heart and a good conscience and a sincere faith. (1 Tim. 1:5)*

All of our spiritual activities, such as praise, worship, prayer, preaching, and teaching are to produce love in the body of believers. Any activity that is not directed toward this goal is idle and useless, according to Paul the Apostle. Our love for God, expressed in our willingness to obey His Word, and our love for people must be improving as the object of our service to Him.

- *Dear friends, let us love one another, for love comes from God. Everyone who loves has been born of God and knows God. (1 John 4:7)*

Definition of the Grace of God from a Kingdom Perspective

In this context, we can define grace as God's provision for the forgiveness of our sins and the empowerment of the Holy Spirit so we can live in obedience to Him. This definition is very crucial because it is in alignment with God's role as King and Judge who demands our obedience. I mentioned in the beginning chapters that the key principle in every kingdom is that the citizens must obey the will of the king, who in turn caters to the needs of the citizens.

- *…and receive from him anything we ask, because we keep his commands and do what pleases him. And this is his command: to believe in the name of his Son, Jesus Christ, and to love one another as he commanded us. (1 John 3:22–23)*

THE LOVE SOLUTION

Scientists have concluded that the chemicals, organs, circuits, and every composition of the human body are wired to be sustained in an environment of love. While we may not be clear on what love truly is, we are aware of its importance in our lives and the lives of others. Most people, however, have been let down and seriously hurt by the very people who claimed to love them. Think about the newlyweds that vowed to love each other till death but divorce a short while after marriage. What about the many broken relationships that exist between races of people, nations, tribes, close friends, and even within families, especially in recent times? These and many more add to our confusion of what love really is. I guess the majority of us feel the same way about the old-time song by Foreigner: "I Want to Know What Love Is." To stress the power of this all-important word that we often throw around, have a read-through of this experiment that was performed years ago.

- Twenty newborn infants were housed in a special facility. They had caregivers who would go in to feed them, bathe them, and change their diapers, but they would do nothing else. The caregivers had been instructed not to look at or touch the babies more than was necessary, and they never spoke to them. All their physical needs were attended to scrupulously however. The environment was kept sterile; the babies were never ill.

The experiment was halted after four months. At least half of the babies had died at that point, and at least two more died even after being rescued and brought into a more normal environment. There was no physiological cause for the babies' deaths; they were all physically very healthy. Before each baby died, there was a period where they would stop verbalizing and trying to engage their caregivers and just stop moving, never crying or changing expression. Death would follow shortly. The babies who had "given up" before being rescued died in the same manner even though they had been removed from the experimental conditions.

The conclusion was that love (nurturing) is a vital need in humans.

The Need To Be Loved

The need to be loved is inherent in all humans. Whether good or evil, all our actions are motivated by this inherent need to be loved. Love is the driving force in our day-to-day lives. Human life is doomed to extinction without love. Think about how most of us came into being—what if your mum and dad didn't get together? Love is so powerful that the consequence of the lack of it is detrimental to us. As a matter of fact, according to research, there are many social and developmental issues associated with children who grow up in broken homes where they are not shown much love. Below is an article sourced from worldimpact.org.

- Inner-city children increasingly grow up in broken households. Fractured and incomplete families perpetuate physical and spiritual poverty. The root cause of poverty and income disparity is undeniably linked to broken family structures. Children growing up in poor, broken households in inner-city America are increasingly exposed to child abuse, teenage pregnancy, alcohol and drug abuse, gang participation, and incarceration. They are also at a higher risk of having broken families of their own. Our nation's inner cities are in need of intact, whole families.

- The American family structure is disintegrating. In 1950, 12 percent of children born in the United States entered into a broken family lacking either a biological mother or father. By 2000, this number had jumped to 60 percent of all children. Unfortunately, the frequency and density of broken families dramatically increases in the impoverished environments of our inner cities. Poor, broken families produce people who are more likely to experience relational and financial poverty as well.

- The fatherless homes that riddle our cities are often toxic environments for our inner-city youth. Fatherless children average significantly higher in our inner cities.

- Broken family environments greatly contribute to the cyclical nature of inner-city poverty.

The Curse of Materialism and the Kingdom Cure

The concept of self-dependency in especially democratic societies has birthed a materialistic world devoid of love. This has caused people to greedily gobble up as many material things as possible so as to be accepted, significant, and respected in the society. The result is increased fear of scarcity, greed, jealousy, hatred, stress, diseases, and death, all of which have a destructive impact in our world.

Real Love Is Missing

The only thing missing in today's world is love. And I am not talking about worldly love such as that which exists between friends (Philia), family (Storge), or partners (Eros), which has created the mess in the first place. We need the God kind of love (agape), unconditional love that is not emotionally driven but decision based. We were created for this kind of love, and that is why we are often left disappointed and never pleased with the world's idea of love. There is no substitute for the lack of the agape love of God in us. Any "love"experienced outside the love of God (Agape) is conditional; it can disappoint at any time. Only God's love "always protects, always trusts, always hopes, always perseveres" (1 Cor. 13:7). God's love for us is not based on who we are or what we do. It is because of who He is.

- *But God demonstrates his own love for us in this: While we were still sinners, Christ died for us. (Rom. 5:8)*

Only God's Love Fulfills

There are several accounts of people who have had near-death experiences. The one thing that most of them testify to is a strong, irresistible, fulfilling sensation of total love and acceptance when they enter the spiritual realm dominated by God. God Himself is love, and His solution to the broken world is His Presence (love). Since we came out of Him, only He (His love) can fulfill us. The presence of the loving nature of God is what makes Heaven, and that's what is required to make earth like Heaven. Jesus is the embodiment of God's love for man. He came to give to the world and show His followers how to love.

The Economic System of God's Government Is Founded on Love

The economic system of God's Kingdom government is designed to portray His infinite love. In the Commonwealth economic system, citizens are empowered to choose sharing over hoarding and giving over greed. This eliminates the problem of materialism and its consequences, such as fear, poverty, and diseases, thereby enhancing a culture of love, peace, and joy.

Every born-again believer has this unconditional love of God shed on their hearts through the Holy Spirit (see Rom. 5:5). The Church therefore, has exactly what the world lacks, and is in desperate need of. By demonstrating this God kind of love (agape) within the body of believers and to those in the world, we challenge the world with a glimpse of the Kingdom of Heaven and are positioned to win the world over into the Kingdom government of God.

- *"By this everyone will know that you are my disciples, if you love one another." (John 13:35)*

TRUE FELLOWSHIP

God is a God of purpose. He has an end purpose to everything He begins. His intent for delivering the children of Israel from captivity in Egypt was to bring them to a promised land where they could serve and worship Him freely. In the same way, salvation offered through Christ is for the end purpose of relationship and fellowship with God and also with other believers.

- *He died for us so that, whether we are awake or asleep, we may live together with him. Therefore encourage one another and build each other up, just as in fact you are doing. (1 Thess. 5:10-11)*

The three things that are eternal in the Godhead (Father, Son, and Holy Spirit) are Fatherhood, Headship, and Fellowship.

God is forever the Father, Head and in an eternal fellowship with the Son in the Holy Spirit. "Fellowship" is the Greek word "Koinonia," meaning having in common or sharing together. The gospel is essentially an invitation to the human race to enter into an eternal fellowship with the Father and the Son in the Holy Spirit.

Unfortunately, most Christians do not realize that there is an end purpose to salvation; therefore, like the Israelites, many wander and often perish in the wilderness of isolation.

Fellowship with God

The Fellowship of the Godhead is the birthplace for God's purposes. Every major decision and act of God concerning the earth involved the fellowship of the Godhead. Let's see some examples:

- *Then God said, "Let us make mankind in our image, in our likeness, so that they may rule over the fish in the sea and the birds in the sky, over the livestock and all the wild animals, and over all the creatures that move along the ground." (Gen. 1:26)*

- *And the LORD God said, "The man has now become like one of us, knowing good and evil. He must not be allowed to reach out his hand and take also from the tree of life and eat, and live forever." (Gen. 3:22)*

- *The LORD said, "If as one people speaking the same language they have begun to do this, then nothing they plan to do will be impossible for them. Come, let us go down and confuse their language so they will not understand each other." (Gen. 11:6–7)*

- *Then I heard the voice of the Lord saying, "Whom shall I send? And who will go for us?" And I said, "Here am I. Send me!" (Is. 6:8)*

We can almost conclude from the scriptures that nothing major will be done on earth by God without the fellowship of the Godhead. This means that we must be in continuous fellowship with God if we are going to be agents of impact on earth. Visions are born out of our fellowship with God, and only visions birthed out of our fellowship with God can be lasting and sure to succeed. Personal ambitions fail or often result in complications because they are born out of the flesh, not through fellowship with the Spirit.

- *Flesh gives birth to flesh, but the Spirit gives birth to spirit. (John 3:6)*

- *for everyone born of God overcomes the world. This is the victory that has overcome the world, even our faith. (1 John 5:4)*

God Does Not Only Have a Son But a Family

We are not only called to a relationship and fellowship with God but also with other believers. God dealt with individuals in the person of Abraham, Isaac, and Jacob in the Old Testament. God enacted a covenant with Abraham and blessed him and through him, blessed his son, Isaac, and grandson, Jacob. Jacob's seed became the nation of Israel. Once the seed of Abraham became a nation, God's focus was shifted from individuals to the well-being of the community of people of Israel, in the same way good parents will not entirely focus on only one child when they have other children to take care of. So whether it was Moses, Aaron, Joshua, judges, kings, prophets, or priests, whenever God dealt with individuals, they were a representative of the whole nation of Israel. In the book of Joshua, the nation of Israel was punished on an account of one man's (Achan's) sin. Also God referred to the entire nation of Israel singularly as "My son, My firstborn" (see Ex. 4:22). The family of Abraham has now been extended to people of all nations and every race who accept the finished work of Jesus on the cross.

- *If you belong to Christ, then you are Abraham's seed, and heirs according to the promise. (Gal. 3:29)*

It is therefore very important to understand that as much as God cares for you, He is also concerned with the general well-being of all the family of believers. Have you ever wondered why the Lord's Prayer is not in the first person? Jesus taught His disciples to include the community of believers in their private prayer to God.

- *"This, then, is how you should pray: 'Our Father in heaven, hallowed be your name.'" (Matt. 6:9)*

This is the essence of the Kingdom government of Heaven. God's actions are motivated by the community, not necessarily individual interests. The focus of God is not just on individuals but also on building a community of people who together represent the King. This is why the concept of Commonwealth is significant in the Kingdom government of Heaven.

- *Jesus answered, "If you want to be perfect, go, sell your possessions and give to the poor, and you will have treasure in heaven. Then come, follow me." (Matt. 19:21)*

The Loss of True Fellowship

True fellowship, however, is a mystery to most believers. The concept of individualism and self-dependency in democratic governments has invaded the church. People hardly laugh or mourn with others as Jesus commanded. The prayer list of a typical modern day believer will reveal the utterly despicable selfishness, greed, and self-centeredness that has penetrated the church. We see ourselves no more than mere independent church members who only gather for worship once or twice a week. An individualistic mindset among believers is what has made many victims of the culture of the world. This, I believe, is one of the reasons why in spite of the large population of Christians in the world, evil is still very prevalent in our societies.

The Fellowship of Believers – The Analogy of the Human Body

Paul the Apostle often used the human body as an analogy to explain the importance of the fellowship of believers. It will not take you long to realize a unique bond in a people that has to depend on each other for survival. This is especially true in most poverty-stricken villages in developing countries. For the most part, the survival of the family or community of people is a function of their reliance on each responsible member to offer support in some way. Nothing strengthens a relationship more than dependency. This is the basis for a covenant. It is a dependency-motivated relationship.

The Community of Believers

To ensure the common union of believers, God, through the Holy Spirit, has also endowed different gifts (healing, miracles, prophecy, teaching) in the "body" that are designed to make us depend on one another for the common good. This strengthens the relationship between believers and makes every believer necessary in the "body." God's collective purpose for the Church will not be realized if we do not function together as the one "body" that we are. We are well aware that the Holy Spirit dwells within us individually, but in 1 Corinthians 3:16, Paul identified the Christians collectively as the temple of the Holy Spirit. It is crucial for the body of Christ to be united in mind and purpose.

Fellowship is Key

The fellowship of believers in the Holy Spirit is the physical expression of the Kingdom government of Heaven on earth. The culture of love within the community of believers enables the fellowshipping believers to withstand the cultural pressure of the world. It is also a powerful tool attracting the people of the world. While we can never force change on the worldly or the nonbeliever, we can influence them to change, and there is no powerful nor influential force on earth than the sight of a people who are able to thrive on the very qualities that are much needed in the world. The existence of the unconditional agape love of God within fellowshipping believers will attract nonbelievers like a magnet. As I pointed out in Chapter 7, it is what all humans on earth are seeking, but they have to see it first before they can be drawn to it.

Principles of Fellowship – Acts 2

Below is a list of principles drawn from the fellowship of the early Church that enabled them to withstand persecution by the Roman authorities and allowed the Church to continue to grow in the midst of it.

- *The obvious and primary place for fellowship was homes of believers. (Acts 2:46)*

- *They were devoted to one another. "Submit to one another out of reverence for Christ" (Eph. 5:21).*

- Acts 2:42 reveals four basic continuing pattern for New Testament living: teaching, fellowship, eating together, and praying together.

To flow in the power of the early church we must have their unity.

10

The Power Of Principles

Every Kingdom Expresses Itself in a Culture

There is a Chinese proverb that goes: "He who claims to be a leader and has no one following is simply taking a walk." It is not enough for people to confess their love and admiration for a leader. They must be willing to live like him/her. A leader is acknowledged when people emulate his/her ways.

- *Follow my example, as I follow the example of Christ. (1 Cor. 11:1)*

Laws and principles are very vital in a kingdom government because kings are acknowledged and honored by their citizens when they obey the king's will (laws and principles). Every kingdom, therefore, expresses itself in a culture. In the Kingdom of God, obedience is better than sacrifice (see 1 Sam 15:22). Citizens are empowered for obedience through the Holy Spirit.

- *who have been chosen according to the foreknowledge of God the Father, through the sanctifying work of the Spirit, to be obedient to Jesus Christ and sprinkled with his blood: Grace and peace be yours in abundance. (1 Pet 1:2)*

Life Is Built on Laws

"Laws" have almost become comparable to a curse word in modern Christianity, but whether we choose to disagree or simply ignore it, the truth is life is built on fundamental natural and spiritual laws. Laws are simply the Creator's directions or instructions for life, as He wants it. Our human nature as free moral agents necessitates the need for laws, because it is the choice to obey or disobey laws but that activates our free will. This is why after presenting His laws to the Israelites, God made the following statement:

- *"This day I call the heavens and the earth as witnesses against you that I have set before you life and death, blessings and curses. Now choose life, so that you and your children may live." (Deut 30:19)*

When God's spiritual laws in the Ten Commandments formed the basis of the constitution, countries such as America thrived until their democratic system of government allowed them to change the foundational laws. The success of everything in life, whether it's personal life or cooperate entities, depends on the engagement of the right laws.

The Law of Sowing and Reaping

I always wondered why it was "mother" and not "father" earth until one day it struck me that it might be in connection with the all-famous universal principle known to many as sowing and reaping, cause and effect, action and reaction. Mother Earth will simply reproduce back to you exactly what you sow in her.

We may have good reasons to blame people, whether they are family, friends, school mates, work mates, etc., for certain failures in our lives, but God ensured that we are solely responsible and accountable for the outcome of our own lives by putting this universal law in place.

- *Do not be deceived: God cannot be mocked. A man reaps what he sows. Whoever sows to please their flesh, from the flesh will reap destruction; whoever sows to please the Spirit, from the Spirit will reap eternal life. Let us not become weary in doing good, for at the proper time we will reap a harvest if we do not give up. (Gal. 6:7–9)*

The question that comes to mind is, why then can't we sow only good seeds (i.e., do the right things) and reap their lasting rewards? The answer is in the story of our first parents (Adam and Eve). Being that we are all their descendants, their act of disobedience in the garden genetically predisposed us to do the wrong things we don't want to; and therefore, suffer the consequences.

- *For I do not do the good I want to do, but the evil I do not want to do—this I keep on doing. (Rom. 7:19)*

Citizens of the Kingdom of Heaven Are Empowered to Sow the Right Seeds

Both the automobile and the airplane as a means of transportation operate under the universal law of gravity. The airplane, however, because of its build and design, is able to engage another law that defies gravity. In the same way, both the believer and the worldly are both liable to the forces of life, but through Christ, the believer is equipped to engage the principles of God, making it possible for the believer to rise above the negative forces of evil.

- *Because through Christ Jesus the law of the Spirit who gives life has set you free from the law of sin and death. (Rom. 8:2)*

In any given situation, we are presented a choice between good and evil. Those in the Kingdom of God are empowered through the indwelling Holy Spirit to make the right choice for their benefit. Those outside the Kingdom of God however, are predisposed to do evil. Citizens of God's kingdom are inclined to do good because we are no longer bear the corrupted nature of Adam.

We descend from Jesus (see 1 Cor.15:45-49). For example, it is more natural for those outside the Kingdom of God to love their friends and hate their enemies. Here's the catch: By sowing hate for their enemies, they reap hatred in their own lives. Kingdom citizens, however, are empowered to sow and reap love to our friends and enemies alike. Also, those outside the Kingdom of God are likely to harbor unforgiveness in their hearts. This means that God cannot also forgive their sins and result is stress-related diseases that may end in death (Rom. 6:23). On the other hand, Kingdom citizens know all too well by the empowerment of the Spirit to apply the following principle:

- *"For if you forgive other people when they sin against you, your heavenly Father will also forgive you. But if you do not forgive others their sins, your Father will not forgive your sins." (Matt. 6:14–15)*

The Kingdom of Heaven Is a Function of Keys (Laws and Principles)

Contrary to what many people think, the Kingdom government of God is a highly ordered system. I mentioned that God is not only a Father but also a King and Judge. Just as in any government, there are procedures to follow to get things done in the Kingdom of Heaven. For example, Jesus taught a specific prayer model as a guideline for His disciples (Matt 6:9).

Personally, I believe the reason why many Christians have failed to bear fruits of the Kingdom of God is because we are ignorant of its keys. The Kingdom government of Heaven is a function of keys (laws and principles), and failure to learn and apply these principles is to be cut off from most of its benefits.

- *my people are destroyed from lack of knowledge. "Because you have rejected knowledge, I also reject you as my priests; because you have ignored the law of your God, I also will ignore your children." (Hos. 4:6)*

Jesus accused the Pharisees of hiding these keys (laws and principles) of the Kingdom of Heaven, thereby preventing the people from entering it. He also went on to say that He would give the keys of the Kingdom of Heaven to His followers (see Matt 16:19). Known by the people of His day as a *Rabbi* (meaning, master teacher), Jesus prioritized teaching and sent the Holy Spirit to continue to teach and empower His followers to apply these keys (laws and principles). Jesus placed a lot of emphasis on the importance of learning and applying the Kingdom laws and principles.

- *"Therefore everyone who hears these words of mine and puts them into practice is like a wise man who built his house on the rock. The rain came down, the streams rose, and the winds blew and beat against that house; yet it did not fall, because it had its foundation on the rock. But everyone who hears these words of mine and does not put them into practice is like a foolish man who built his house on sand.*

The rain came down, the streams rose, and the winds blew and beat against that house, and it fell with a great crash." *(Matt 7:24-27)*

The Seed Principle of the Word

A principle is an established truth that when applied, guarantees the expected result, just as a mango seed is guaranteed to grow into a mango fruit if sown in soil and watered. God, the author of life, has provided principles of His Kingdom government, which, when we apply them to our lives, guarantee the best and ideal life as He designed it.

In Luke 8:11, Jesus refers to the Word (laws and principles) of God as a seed. Just as a seed sown in the soil and watered constantly bears fruit in time, so it is with working the laws and principles of the Kingdom of Heaven. While we may not realize instant results or may not even understand how it works, we will—with patience, consistency, and endurance—reap the benefits in due time.

- *Let us not become weary in doing good, for at the proper time we will reap a harvest if we do not give up. (Gal 6:9)*

Sometimes we see people around us who have become fruitful in many areas of their lives. They have great marriages; are successful, healthy, and happy; and have well-trained and responsible children, etc. All these are beautiful and attractive fruits we admire about such people, but what we do not realize is that all the wonderful things we see going for them didn't just happen overnight. They first had to sow seeds (principles) in all of those areas and then fight the test of time and harsh conditions (opposition) to be fruitful (successful).

The Bible is the Creator's Manual

The Bible is not a religious book. It is the Creator's manual for life as He designed it. Wrapped in the stories of God's dealings with people such as the patriarchs, prophets, judges, kings and so on, are His laws and principles that address all areas of life. Jesus came to perfect these Kingdom laws and principles and empower us through the Holy Spirit so we will be able to apply them.

- *"For the law was given through Moses; grace and truth came through Jesus Christ" (Joh. 1:17)*

What separates the worldly from the heavenly?

The application of the laws and principles of the Kingdom of Heaven distinguishes the lifestyle of citizens of the Kingdom of Heaven from the worldly. The worldly live by their senses (sow to the flesh) and therefore, reap destruction, while those in the Kingdom of God live by faith (sow to the spirit) and reap eternal life.

- *Whoever sows to please their flesh, from the flesh will reap destruction; whoever sows to please the Spirit, from the Spirit will reap eternal life. (Gal. 6:8)*

The Church (God's government agency) is called to be the light of the world and the salt of the earth. It is our engagement of these revealed principles and laws, a mystery to those in the world, that will set us apart and position us as citizens of God's kingdom and true rulers of the earth. Remember that all our supplies on earth from the Kingdom of God are wrapped up in our obedience to His Word (laws and principles).

- *But seek first his kingdom and his righteousness, and all these things will be given to you as well. (Matt. 6:33)*

- *Keep this Book of the Law always on your lips; meditate on it day and night, so that you may be careful to do everything written in it. Then you will be prosperous and successful. (Joshua 1:8)*

- *My son, pay attention to what I say; turn your ear to my words. Do not let them out of your sight, keep them within your heart; for they are life to those who find them and health to one's whole body. (Prov. 4:20–22)*

Below are some Kingdom keys (laws and principles) for Kingdom citizens most of which is derived from the gospels. Please be aware that all of these principles can be summed up in love for God and people. Love is the fulfillment of the law.

LAW OF CITIZENSHIP	THE PRINCIPLE OF LOVE
Jesus answered, "Very truly I tell you, no one can enter the kingdom of God unless they are born of water and the Spirit." (John 3:5)	*Jesus replied: "Love the Lord your God with all your heart and with all your soul and with all your mind." This is the first and greatest commandment. And the second is like it: "Love your neighbor as yourself." (Matt. 22:37–39)*
KEY TO KINGDOM SUPPLY	**PRINCIPLE OF INCREASE**
But seek first his kingdom and his righteousness, and all these things will be given to you as well. (Matt. 6:33)	*"His master replied, 'Well done, good and faithful servant! You have been faithful with a few things; I will put you in charge of many things. Come and share your master's happiness!'" (Matt. 25:23)*
PRINCIPLE OF COMMENDATION	**PRINCIPLE OF MERCY**
But whoever disowns me before others, I will disown before my Father in heaven. (Matt 10:32–33)	*Blessed are the merciful, for they will be shown mercy. (Matt. 5:7)*

PRINCIPLE OF PRAYER

"And when you pray, do not be like the hypocrites, for they love to pray standing in the synagogues and on the street corners to be seen by others. Truly I tell you, they have received their reward in full. But when you pray, go into your room, close the door and pray to your Father, who is unseen. Then your Father, who sees what is done in secret, will reward you. And when you pray, do not keep on babbling like pagans, for they think they will be heard because of their many words. Do not be like them, for your Father knows what you need before you ask him.

This, then, is how you should pray: 'Our Father in heaven, hallowed be your name,

your kingdom come, your will be done, on earth as it is in heaven.

Give us today our daily bread.

And forgive us our debts, as we also have forgiven our debtors.

And lead us not into temptation, but deliver us from the evil one.'"

(Matt. 6:5–13)

"Therefore I tell you, whatever you ask for in prayer, believe that you have received it, and it will be yours. And when you stand praying, if you hold anything against anyone, forgive them, so that your Father in heaven may forgive you your sins."

(Mark 11:24–25)

PRINCIPLE OF GIVING

"Be careful not to practice your righteousness in front of others to be seen by them. If you do, you will have no reward from your Father in heaven. So when you give to the needy, do not announce it with trumpets, as the hypocrites do in the synagogues and on the streets, to be honored by others. Truly I tell you, they have received their reward in full. But when you give to the needy, do not let your left hand know what your right hand is doing, so that your giving may be in secret. Then your Father, who sees what is done in secret, will reward you." (Matt. 6:1–4)

Remember this: Whoever sows sparingly will also reap sparingly, and whoever sows generously will also reap generously. Each of you should give what you have decided in your heart to give, not reluctantly or under compulsion, for God loves a cheerful giver. And God is able to bless you abundantly, so that in all things at all times, having all that you need, you will abound in every good work. As it is written: "They have freely scattered their gifts to the poor; their righteousness endures forever." Now he who supplies seed to the sower and bread for food will also supply and increase your store of seed and will enlarge the harvest of your righteousness. You will be enriched in every way so that you can be generous on every occasion, and through us your generosity will result in thanksgiving to God.

(2 Cor. 9:6–11)

PRINCIPLE OF WORSHIP

Yet a time is coming and has now come when the true worshipers will worship the Father in the Spirit and in truth, for they are the kind of worshipers the Father seeks. (John 4:23)

PRINCIPLE OF AGREEMENT

"Again, truly I tell you that if two of you on earth agree about anything they ask for, it will be done for them by my Father in heaven. For where two or three gather in my name, there am I with them." (Matt. 6:19–20)

PRINCIPLE OF GREATNESS

The greatest among you will be your servant. For those who exalt themselves will be humbled, and those who humble themselves will be exalted. (Matt. 23:11–12)

Therefore anyone who sets aside one of the least of these commands and teaches others accordingly will be called least in the kingdom of heaven, but whoever practices and teaches these commands will be called great in the kingdom of heaven. (Matt. 5:19)

LAW OF OATHS

"Again, you have heard that it was said to the people long ago, 'Do not break your oath, but fulfill to the Lord the vows you have made.' But I tell you, do not swear an oath at all: either by heaven, for it is God's throne; or by the earth, for it is his footstool; or by Jerusalem, for it is the city of the Great King. And do not swear by your head, for you cannot make even one hair white or black. All you need to say is simply 'Yes' or 'No'; anything beyond this comes from the evil one." (Matt. 5:33-37)

PRINCIPLE OF FAITH

"If you can?" said Jesus. "Everything is possible for one who believes." (Mark 9:23)

He replied, "Because you have so little faith. Truly I tell you, if you have faith as small as a mustard seed, you can say to this mountain, 'Move from here to there,' and it will move. Nothing will be impossible for you."

(Matt. 17:20)

PRINCIPLE OF FORGIVENESS

For if you forgive other people when they sin against you, your heavenly Father will also forgive you. But if you do not forgive others their sins, your Father will not forgive your sins. (Matt 6:14–15)

PRINCIPLE OF MARRIAGE

"It has been said, 'Anyone who divorces his wife must give her a certificate of divorce.' But I tell you that anyone who divorces his wife, except for sexual immorality, makes her the victim of adultery, and anyone who marries a divorced woman commits adultery." (Matt. 5:31–32)

Husbands, love your wives, just as Christ loved the church and gave himself up for her to make her holy, cleansing her by the washing with water through the word, and to present her to himself as a radiant church, without stain or wrinkle or any other blemish, but holy and blameless. In this same way, husbands ought to love their wives as their own bodies. He who loves his wife loves himself. After all, no one ever hated their own body, but they feed and care for their body, just as Christ does the church— for we are members of his body. "For this reason a man will leave his father and mother and be united to his wife, and the two will become one flesh." This is a profound mystery—but I am talking about Christ and the church. However, each one of you also must love his wife as he loves himself, and the wife must respect her husband. (Eph. 5:25–33)

"You have heard that it was said, 'You shall not commit adultery.' But I tell you that anyone who looks at a woman lustfully has already committed adultery with her in his heart." (Matt. 5:27–28)

LAW OF TOLERANCE

"You have heard that it was said, 'Eye for eye, and tooth for tooth.' But I tell you, do not resist an evil person. If anyone slaps you on the right cheek, turn to them the other cheek also. And if anyone wants to sue you and take your shirt, hand over your coat as well. If anyone forces you to go one mile, go with them two miles. Give to the one who asks you, and do not turn away from the one who wants to borrow from you. (Matt 5:38-42)

"You have heard that it was said, 'Love your neighbor and hate your enemy.' But I tell you, love your enemies and pray for those who persecute you, that you may be children of your Father in heaven. He causes his sun to rise on the evil and the good, and sends rain on the righteous and unrighteous. If you love those who love you, what reward will you get? Are not even the tax collectors doing that? And if you greet only your own people, what are you doing more than others? Do not even pagans do that? Be perfect, therefore, as your heavenly Father is perfect." (Matt 5:43–48)

PRINCIPLE OF RECEIVING

Ask and it will be given to you; seek and you will find; knock and the door will be opened to you. For everyone who asks receives; the one who seeks finds; and to the one who knocks, the door will be opened. (Matt 7:7–8)

PRINCIPLE OF BEARING FRUIT

Remain in me, as I also remain in you. No branch can bear fruit by itself; it must remain in the vine. Neither can you bear fruit unless you remain in me. "I am the vine; you are the branches. If you remain in me and I in you, you will bear much fruit; apart from me you can do nothing. If you do not remain in me, you are like a branch that is thrown away and withers; such branches are picked up, thrown into the fire and burned. If you remain in me and my words remain in you, ask whatever you wish, and it will be done for you. This is to my Father's glory, that you bear much fruit, showing yourselves to be my disciples. (John 15:4–8)

PRINCIPLE OF RELATIONSHIPS

You have heard that it was said to the people long ago, 'You shall not murder, and anyone who murders will be subject to judgment.' But I tell you that anyone who is angry with a brother or sister, will be subject to judgment. Again, anyone who says to a brother or sister, 'Raca,' is answerable to the court. And anyone who says, 'You fool!' will be in danger of the fire of hell. Therefore, if you are offering your gift at the altar and there remember that your brother or sister has something against you, leave your gift there in front of the altar. First go and be reconciled to them; then come and offer your gift. Settle matters quickly with your adversary who is taking you to court. Do it while you are still together on the way, or your adversary may hand you over to the judge, and the judge may hand you over to the officer, and you may be thrown into prison. (Matt. 5:21–26)

PRINCIPLE OF HONOUR

"Anyone who welcomes you welcomes me, and anyone who welcomes me welcomes the one who sent me. Whoever welcomes a prophet as a prophet will receive a prophet's reward, and whoever welcomes a righteous person as a righteous person will receive a righteous person's reward. And if anyone gives even a cup of cold water to one of these little ones who is my disciple, truly I tell you, that person will certainly not lose their reward."

(Matt. 10:40–44)

PRINCIPLE OF FASTING

"When you fast, do not look somber as the hypocrites do, for they disfigure their faces to show others they are fasting. Truly I tell you, they have received their reward in full. But when you fast, put oil on your head and wash your face, so that it will not be obvious to others that you are fasting, but only to your Father, who is unseen; and your Father, who sees what is done in secret, will reward you."

(Matt. 6:16–18)

God's Kingdom Government Vs. Worldly Governments

The power of exposure

Back when I was a teenager, there was one TV series that got me to question and seek answers as to why life would be so unfair. Every session of MTV Cribs, a program that provided a stage for music, movie, and sports stars to show off their possessions, left me almost depressed. I would not say that I come from a poor family, because I lived in Africa long enough to know my living standards were far above many that were considered poor. But the TV show did a good job of making me realize that we were still far from what would be considered rich or wealthy in the Western world. Its impact on me was so great that I started thinking about what I could do to live like those celebrities. Over time I came to realize this intriguing truth: that humans usually adapt to any situation until they are exposed to something they deem better.

- *But the people refused to listen to Samuel. "No!" they said. "We want a king over us. **Then we will be like all the other nations**, with a king to lead us and to go out before us and fight our battles." (1 Sam. 8:19–20)*

God asked Abraham to get out and number the stars as a sign of his descendants; God also revealed Joseph's future to him in his dreams long before he became a governor in Egypt. Jesus Himself, for the joy of the glory set before Him, endured the cross (see Heb 12:2). The entire Bible is filled with prophecies of events, some of which have already happened and some still yet to occur. **My point is, exposure is the pressure required to thrust humans to new experiences.**

The Three Major Groups of People

We were born and raised under worldly governing systems that function on principles and laws sourced from fallen men and not from the wisdom of the Creator.

The result is three major groups of people in the world:

- There are those who feel trapped and are groaning because of the corrupted worldly governing systems but do not "*see*" a way out of it.

- There is a majority who has accepted what is because they do not "*see*" any better. The present state of things is their only reality.

- Then a minority who "*see*" what could be but do not "*see*" themselves equipped enough to make the changes.

What is common to all the three groups of people is the inability to "*see*."

Jesus Addressed Our Inability to "See"

Jesus addressed our inability to "see" (not just physically) as one of our problems.

- *"The Spirit of the Lord is on me, because he has anointed me to proclaim good news to the poor. He has sent me to proclaim freedom for the prisoners and recovery of sight for the blind, to set the oppressed free." (Luke 4:18)*

We have succumbed to defective worldly governing systems created by fallen men but cannot "see" our way out of it. My goal in this chapter is to expose some of the defects in worldly governments and with the help of the Holy Spirit help you to "see" or understand the new order of life, the governing system of God that was lost in the Garden of Eden but brought back by Jesus.

- *Have nothing to do with the fruitless deeds of darkness, but rather expose them. (Eph. 5:11)*

My objective is to help you detach from these defective worldly governments and hook up to the all-sufficient eternal Kingdom government of God.

Before that, I want to recap the following;

Summary

➢ God created man to govern the earth (Gen 1:26).

➢ The most powerful controlling force on earth is government.

➢ God Himself believes in proper government because the right government produces stability, peace, order, growth, and protection for His creation.

➢ To enable man to fulfill the responsibility of government, the Creator put His very nature (image and likeness) in man.

➤ The principal function of government is to enhance peaceful coexistence and to orchestrate the wise use of the earth's resources for the benefit of all citizens.

➤ God's nature (image and likeness) in man was lost through rebellion by Adam and Eve; therefore, the right and proper government was lost.

➤ Consequently, most people all over the world have been victims of injustice and inequality as broken human relationships impact the misuse, misdirection and mismanagement of resources.

➤ The greatest challenge of all humanity since the fall of Adam and Eve has been dissatisfaction with government.

➤ People all over the world have demanded transparency, protection, justice, equality, and honesty from their government.

➤ Jesus came to restore God's nature (image and likeness) back into man so as to enable the right and proper government (dominion) of the earth.

➤ The Church (assembly of believers) is the product of the work of Jesus; therefore, endowed with the nature (image and likeness) of God to once again govern or dominate the earth as instructed by God in the book of Genesis.

The following scripture necessitates the need for God's righteous government through the body of believers or the Church on earth:

- *He makes nations great, and destroys them; he enlarges nations, and disperses them.* **He deprives the leaders of the earth of their reason; he makes them wander in a trackless waste. They grope in darkness with no light; he makes them stagger like drunkards***. (Job 12:23–25)*

I hope by now you are convinced as I am that the earth as we know it, is headed for destruction if God's ordained "light of the world" (the Church) does not begin to gain more influence in our societies by functioning as an independent kingdom government of God on earth.

One Earth, Two Worlds

There are two words that I want to bring your attention to: "Earth" and "World." These two words are often used interchangeably, but they are remarkably different in meaning. Biblically, the earth refers to the physical, natural planet, which includes the land, sea, plants, trees, animals, and so on. Let's say it is everything God created from days 1 to 5 as the book of Genesis recounts.

The "world", however, refers to the governing systems of the earth. For example, the "world of sports", the "world of politics", the "world of entertainment," and so on. Governments control the "world," and the "world" controls what happens on the earth.

The earth was created to be controlled by the "world of Heaven" through the Kingdom government of God. The earth (physical planet) itself is still partially subjected to God's Kingdom because it doesn't have the free will to decide otherwise. But, it is suffering from the effects of the "world" of the kingdom of darkness manifested through man's own government, due to the rejection and rebellion against the Kingdom government of Heaven on earth. In effect, there are two worlds (governing systems) battling for the earth: the Kingdom of Heaven on earth manifested through the true Church and the kingdom of darkness manifested through any other form of government.

Jesus said He is the light and truth of the world, meaning that any governing system that is not built on Him or His principles is operating in darkness; and therefore, headed for destruction. In fact, He came to save the "world" of darkness that was condemned (John 3:16).

The Power of The Environment

Governments create and set the environment for human development, and while we may underestimate its effects, the environment is a powerful influencing force on earth. Humans are compelled to be products of our environment.

- *Do not be misled: "Bad company corrupts good character."*
  (1 Cor. 15:33)

I had the privilege of spending some time with detainees from a Juvenile Justice Center. An interesting observation I made was that while detained, these teenagers were more open to, and made efforts to change for the better. I later found out from the staff that approximately 98% of detainees were likely to commit the same offenses only to return again. As a matter of fact, one of the boys testified to this truth when he stated "how hard it is to stay changed while out." According to him, he is a victim and does not have what it takes to fight the force of an environment/culture that directly or indirectly promotes and glorifies rebellion, drugs, and sex among teenagers.

If God is interested in our lifestyle on earth, then God must be in the position to create and set the environment for human behavior development. That can happen only when His representatives, the body of believers (the church) begin to exercise our authority as an independent government agency.

How Can The Church Takeover The Government of The Earth?

It is said that in order to check the mental progress of a psychiatric patient, the psychiatrists perform a simple test by asking the patient to mop out water while a tap is allowed to run on the floor. A progress is indicated if the patient does not continue in the attempt to get rid of the water by mopping it out, but goes on to remove the source of the problem by closing the tap.

To effectively solve the problems of this world, we cannot just be addressing its effects; we must remove the source of the problems. Whether it has to do with the economy, education, business, families, media, entertainment, or religion, the government administrates all these areas that influence our lives on earth. We have to switch governments. We must stop participating in worldly governments and start engaging the governing systems of the Kingdom of Heaven through the church. Remember that the only reason why these worldly governing systems exist is because we give it life by participating in it; once we disengage and disciple people out of it, it will die out.

The 7 Pillars

- *Wisdom has built her house; she has set up its seven pillars. (Prov. 9:1)*

- *By wisdom the LORD laid the earth's foundations, by understanding he set the heavens in place. (Prov. 3:19)*

- *His intent was that now, through the church, the manifold wisdom of God should be made known to the rulers and authorities in the heavenly realms, according to his eternal purpose that he accomplished in Christ Jesus our Lord. (Eph. 3:10–11)*

We can pick up two main things from the scriptures above.

Firstly, God created the earth and, by His wisdom, set up seven pillars (spheres of influence). They are family, business, media, education, economy, spirituality, and entertainment. Every one of these is a major influencer and a determining factor of our culture or lifestyle on earth.

Secondly, according to Ephesians 3:10, God's intent or purpose in the last days is to reveal His wisdom through the Church. In other words, the true Church founded on Christ is to be the foundation for these seven spheres of influence in our societies. The Church must be represented in all of these areas to effectively influence the world. The expansion of the Kingdom government of Heaven rests in the ability of the Church to function as an independent government, where it will be in the position to administer or regulate the operation of these seven influencers in the world.

- *In the last days the mountain of the LORD's temple will be established as the highest of the mountains; it will be exalted above the hills, and all nations will stream to it. Many peoples will come and say, "Come, let us go up to the mountain of the LORD, to the temple of the God of Jacob. He will teach us his ways, so that we may walk in his paths." The law will go out from Zion, the word of the Lord from Jerusalem. (Is. 2:2–3)*

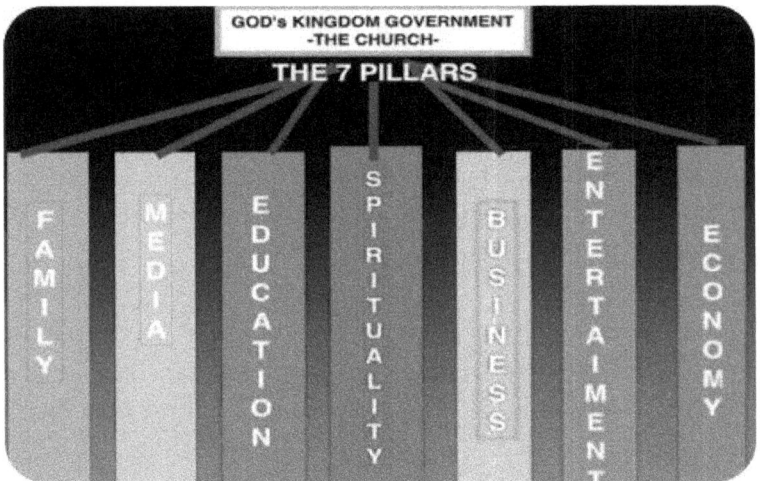

GOD's KINGDOM GOVERNMENT -THE CHURCH-

THE 7 PILLARS

FAMILY | MEDIA | EDUCATION | SPIRITUALITY | BUSINESS | ENTERTAIMENT | ECONOMY

The Need for the Church to Operate Independently of the World

I have heard many believers suggest that the best way to influence and effect change in the world is to participate or be involved in the politics of the world. Their idea is, if they could become leaders in the field of politics, they will be in the position to instigate the legislation of only laws that are in agreement with God's will. While the intention is good and it seems like a good idea, it does not work. Just as we do not advise our good, well-trained children to marry wicked people in an attempt to change them, the idea to participate in worldly politics with that objective in mind has not and will not work. Worldly governments, especially in democracy, is built on a foundation of people, most of which have not submitted wholly to God's will. Therefore, they will prevent and resist anyone that represents the principles and values of God's Kingdom. Bear in mind that in a governing system such as democracy, the power is in the hands of the people not an individual, even if the individual is a government leader. **If the hearts of the people do not change, no one can alter the systems they uphold.**

Why Participating in Worldly Politics Will Not Work

Here are more reasons why the concept of joining worldly politics to effect change is ineffective. First, no matter how good your intentions may be, you cannot build on a foundation of a system set up by fallen men. The Church must be the foundation of all governing systems because it is the pillar and foundation for truth (see 1 Tim. 3:15). Secondly, there's a demand to conform to any governing system before one can be accepted, so a believer may have to compromise their values in order to be welcomed in worldly politics. Let's remember that friendship with the world makes an enemy of God (1 John 2:15).

Come Out of Them

This is why God's instruction has always been: "Come out of them." God's intention is to first have a people set apart under His own government and then invite the world over from theirs into His. Children of God have nothing to learn from those who walk in darkness. Worldly people use worldly governments as an avenue to implement their worldview. Believers must express and uphold only the worldview of the Kingdom government of God.

- *See, I have taught you decrees and laws as the Lord my God commanded me, so that you may follow them in the land you are entering to take possession of it. Observe them carefully, for this will show your wisdom and understanding to the nations, who will hear about all these decrees and say, "Surely this great nation is a wise and understanding people." What other nation is so great as to have their gods near them the way the Lord our God is near us whenever we pray to him? And what other nation is so great as to have such righteous decrees and laws as this body of laws I am setting before you today? (Deut. 4: 5–8)*

- *Then I heard another voice from heaven say: "'Come out of her, my people,' so that you will not share in her sins, so that you will not receive any of her plagues." (Rev. 18:4)*

The Only Foundation for Government on Earth

If Jesus is the chief cornerstone (see Eph. 2:20), then His Kingdom government must be centered on Him. And that is exactly one of the reasons why He came—to show us how to operate in His Kingdom, which is independent of the worldly systems. Let's remember that He said, "…no man can see the Kingdom of God unless they are born of the spirit" (John 3:5). Any government operation on earth that is not Holy Spirit-led does not represent God's Kingdom government, and believers or Christians cannot involve ourselves in any way or support such governments. Involving the Church with the politics of the world defeats the very purpose of the Church. Democracy is simply a system of the collective expression of self-will. Through Jesus the self-will of believers is crucified so we can do the will of God representing His Kingdom government on earth.

What if governing authorities of worldly governments claim to be born again?

First of all, if they are truly born again, they should not be involved in the worldly politics, because as I mentioned, its foundation is built on the will of men and not of God. The place of a true born-again Believer should be in God's Kingdom government in the Church. The greatest in God's Kingdom government are those that teach as well as obey His laws. All believers are equally vice governors, but the leaders in the Kingdom government of Heaven are the anointed interpreters and doers of God's laws and principles.

- *Therefore anyone who sets aside one of the least of these commands and teaches others accordingly will be called least in the kingdom of heaven, but whoever practices and teaches these commands will be called great in the kingdom of heaven. (Matt. 5:19)*

Taking Responsibility for the Earth

The oppression and domination of men by other men who capitalize on the poor, the disadvantaged, and the weak in our societies is the result of the defective image (nature) of man and, consequently, the misapplication of God's original mandate. Man was created in God's image to dominate or control everything on earth but never other men. The only people God can trust with His mandate to govern the earth without oppressing and abusing the weak is a people who possess His image. Through the sacrificial death on the cross, Jesus paid the price for our original image (God's image) to be restored in a people (the Church) who pledge their allegiance to Him as King. God therefore, has empowered and positioned the Church to act on His behalf on earth. As I mentioned in previous chapters, a King's responsibility is to provide for the citizens while it is the duty of citizens to obey the King. God seeks to meet the needs of humanity, especially those disadvantaged through His Church.

- *"Then the King will say to those on his right, 'Come, you who are blessed by my Father; take your inheritance, the kingdom prepared for you since the creation of the world. For I was hungry and you gave me something to eat, I was thirsty and you gave me something to drink, I was a stranger and you invited me in, I needed clothes and you clothed me, I was sick and you looked after me, I was in prison and you came to visit me.' Then the righteous will answer him, 'Lord, when did we see you hungry and feed you, or thirsty and give you something to drink? When did we see you a stranger and invite you in, or needing clothes and clothe you? When did we see you sick or in prison and go to visit you?' The King will reply, 'Truly I tell you, whatever you did for one of the least of these brothers and sisters of mine, you did for me.'"* (Matt. 25:34–40)

Who You Acknowledge as Your Source Is Your God

It is said that in order to gain the trust of citizens in some communist government countries, children are asked to pray to God for a candy; on getting nothing, the children are again asked to pray, this time asking the state government for candy. They are then given the candy and told that God does not exist, the state government is their god. This reminds me of a story in the Bible where God used Paul and Barnabas to heal a crippled man. It records that the people saw them as gods and almost proceeded to worship them.

- *When the crowd saw what Paul had done, they shouted in the Lycaonian language, "The gods have come down to us in human form!" Barnabas they called Zeus, and Paul they called Hermes because he was the chief speaker. (Acts 14:11–12)*

My point is people are likely to submit to and make gods out of whatever they perceive to be their provider. This is why God cannot trust any person or group to govern the earth that doesn't represent Him. For this reason, the true Church (representing God) is equipped to take full responsibility for the weak and disadvantaged people on earth. Jesus' command to His disciples to preach the gospel to all creation (see Mark 16:15) takes us back to man's original mandate given by God in the book of Genesis.

God's Kingdom Government Demands Mind Renewal

"Govern" means to control or guide; "ment" is from the latin word "mente" meaning mind. Any system that controls people's minds and actions is a government. Government engages the mind, hence it is impossible to experience the Kingdom government of Heaven without renewing your mind. Here is why Jesus' first Word was "repent." To "repent" means to change your mind and actions. It is not necessarily an emotional experience but a willful act. The best example to describe this act of repentance is driving on the road and realizing you are heading the wrong way, so you make a U-turn to travel the right way.

- *Do not conform to the pattern of this world, but be transformed by the renewing of your mind. Then you will be able to test and approve what God's will is—his good, pleasing and perfect will. (Rom. 12:2)*

We have to get rid of all we know and be open to a new thinking pattern altogether to be to able operate in the Kingdom government of Heaven. Jesus put it best:

- *Truly I tell you, anyone who will not receive the kingdom of God like a little child will never enter it." (Mark 10:15)*

You would think that righteous Jesus would rebuke His disciples because of sin, but interestingly enough, each time Jesus reprimanded them, it had to do with their faith. **Faith therefore, is a prerequisite for Kingdom life**. It is impossible to engage the lifestyle of the Kingdom government of Heaven without faith.

How Do You Define Reality?

The fact that we may view the present state of the world as reality does not necessarily mean that it is. I am sure people who lived in earlier centuries could not even conceive of the idea of life as it is now. Many aspects of life viewed as reality were once inconceivable by the generations before us. The things we have adopted as part of our normal life was abnormal. For example, there was a time when horses were the main form of transport, but cars were introduced and became the norm or "reality." There were times when home school was the norm until the public educational system was introduced. How about the impact of the Industrial Revolution, which birthed the 9am–5pm lifestyle. It is almost impossible to imagine that there was a time when people did not run on a 9 to 5 schedule. The Kingdom government of Heaven is a complete social transformation. It impacts our lifestyle and how we see life altogether. The great news about it—it is the only true measure of reality of life as designed by the Creator.

- *Since, then, you have been raised with Christ, set your hearts on things above, where Christ is, seated at the right hand of God. Set your minds on things above, not on earthly things. For you died, and your life is now hidden with Christ in God. (Col 3:1-3)*

The table below compares the operation of worldly governments versus the government of the Kingdom of God.

	ALL EARTHLY or WORLDLY GOVERNMENTS	GOD's GOVERNMENT ON EARTH -THE TRUE CHURCH
System of Government	Democracy, Communism etc	Kingdom (Matt 3:2) (Psa 103:19)(Luke 17:20)
Source	Earth (natural)	Heaven(Spiritual), (Luke 17:21)(John 18:36)
Laws	Governmental Constitution	Bible (Luke 6:46)(Matt 7:21)
Operation	by Sense knowledge(Intellect+Logic)	By faith and discernment (Rom 1:17)(2 Cor 4:18)
Leader/Authority	Elected (by the people)	King Jesus (John 18:37) (Isa 9:6)
Style of Leadership	Authoritarian, Oppressive	Service and Sacrifice (Matt 23:11) (Man 5:19)
Entrance	Birth, Naturalisation	By Spiritual Birth, born again (John 3:3)
Citizens Relationship	Citizens	Family&Citizen (1 John 3:9).(Heb 2:11)(Rom 12:5)
Economy	Capitalism(Focus on individual success)	Commonwealth (focus on the needy)(Acts 2:45)
Citizens lifestyle	Fear / Greed / Conformers	By love (John 13:35)(Matt 22:39)(Abundance/uniquenes
Healthcare	Medicine	Hands on healing (Mark 16:18) (James 5:4)
Defence/ Security	Military	Angels (Psa 91:11) (Heb 1:14) (Matt 26:53) (Jos 5:14) (Acts 12:11)
Duration	Confined to Life on earth	During & After life (1 Pet 4:5)(Matt 19:29)
Source of resources	Income taxes	Kingdom commonwealth
Priority	Provision	Obedience to the king (Deu 28)(Matt 6:33),(Jos1-8)

THE PROPHESY WAS THAT HE WAS BRINGING A GOVERNMENT ON HIS SHOULDERS (Isa 9:6). WHAT JESUS(THE HEAD)LEFT BEHIND WAS THE CHURCH(HIS BODY)(Matt 16:18)(Col 1:18) THE CHURCH IS AND MOST FUNCTION AS A GOVERNMENT(KINGDOM). The Church leaders are the Ministers, the born again congregation are the citizens and Jesus is the King. DAN 7:27 ; REV 11:15 ; REV 5:10

System of Government

The most distinctive feature of worldly governments, whether democracy or communism, is that it takes into account the will of men. Governing laws are a reflection of man's will and not necessarily God's will.

The Kingdom government of God, however, rules by the sovereign Word of God. It does NOT take into account the will or opinions of men. Citizens submit to and obey the will of God.

- *"Not everyone who says to me, 'Lord, Lord,' will enter the kingdom of heaven, but only the one who does the will of my Father who is in heaven." (Matt. 7:21)*

Source

Worldly governments are sourced from and confined to the earth. The laws and principles are limited to the understanding of how things work on earth. For example, scientific, psychological and various other factors can be considered to legalize homosexuality, abortion etc. The Bible connotes engaging its laws and principles as sowing to the flesh, which has destructive implications.

- *Whoever sows to please their flesh, from the flesh will reap destruction….(Gal 6:8)*

Principles and laws of the Kingdom government of God are sourced from a spiritual realm (Heaven). The Bible connotes the engagement of its principles as sowing to the Spirit which results in eternal life.

- *….. whoever sows to please the Spirit, from the Spirit will reap eternal life. (Gal. 6:8)*

Laws and Principles

Governing laws of worldly governments are sourced from what is known as a governmental constitution. These are the fundamental principles according to which the state is governed. In democratic countries, these laws are primarily the result of majority votes by the citizens.

In the Kingdom government of God, the Bible is the constitution and the source of all governing laws and principles. Laws are not up to be debated or voted on. The duty of citizens is to obey.

- *"Not everyone who says to me, 'Lord, Lord,' will enter the kingdom of heaven, but only the one who does the will of my Father who is in heaven. (Matt 7:21)*

Operation

Worldly governing systems are built on sense knowledge. This mode of operation completely removes any dependency on God.

The importance of legislating laws according to God's Word becomes irrelevant.

The kingdom government of God is built on faith. God gives us faith when we get born again because it is a requirement to live in His Kingdom. This system of government operates according to how things work in Heaven. Its superior laws and principles may not make sense to our natural mind but the citizens obey by trust and faith in the King.

- *For we live by faith, not by sight. (2 Cor. 5:7)*

Leadership

Leaders are usually temporarily appointed or elected to power by majority votes in most worldly governments.

In the Kingdom government of God, Jesus is appointed to be King forever. Appointment of leaders within His government agency (the Church) must be Holy Spirit-led.

- *"You will conceive and give birth to a son, and you are to call him Jesus. He will be great and will be called the Son of the Most High. The Lord God will give him the throne of his father David, and he will reign over Jacob's descendants forever; his kingdom will never end." (Luke 1:31–33)*

Style of Leadership

The style of leadership by worldly government authorities is usually authoritarian and oppressive. Elected chief citizens usually despise the average citizen.

In the Kingdom government of God, leaders are to be servants of the citizens. The King of Heaven Himself led an exemplary life of leadership through service.

- *Jesus called them together and said, "You know that the rulers of the Gentiles lord it over them, and their high officials exercise authority over them. Not so with you. Instead, whoever wants to become great among you must be your servant, and whoever wants to be first must be your slave—just as the Son of Man did not come to be served, but to serve, and to give his life as a ransom for many." (Matt 20:25–28)*

How You Become a Citizen

Citizenship is by natural birth or naturalization in worldly governments.

The Kingdom government of God is spiritual, therefore, you can only become a citizen by spiritual birth. This occurs when one repents, confesses Jesus as Lord. Baptism of water and Spirit then follows.

- *Jesus replied, "Very truly I tell you, no one can see the kingdom of God unless they are born again." "How can someone be born when they are old?" Nicodemus asked. "Surely they cannot enter a second time into their mother's womb to be born!" Jesus answered, "Very truly I tell you, no one can enter the kingdom of God unless they are born of water and the Spirit. Flesh gives birth to flesh, but the Spirit gives birth to spirit." (John 3:3–6)*

How Citizens Relate

Except in the case of a biological relation, people under a common worldly government can only relate as citizens. This means that in the absence of a national threat that usually brings citizens together for a common cause, they generally live separate, independent lives without care or support for each other.

Citizens of the Kingdom government of God are not only related as citizens but also as members of the family of God. They are born again by Spirit of God. This enables people of different biological families, color, gender, and all nations to exercise love for each other in a manner that those in worldly governments are unable to.

- *Consequently, you are no longer foreigners and strangers, but fellow citizens with God's people and also members of his household. (Eph. 2:19)*

- *But our citizenship is in heaven. And we eagerly await a Savior from there, the Lord Jesus Christ. (Phil. 3:20)*

Lifestyle of The Citizens

Worldly governments systems are dominated by fear. Citizens live in constant fear of scarcity because it is a system that heavily relies on them for continuous supply. Fear of scarcity is the root of greed, covetousness, hate, war, confusion, stress, and diseases.

The dominant forces in the Kingdom government of God are love, peace, and joy. The supplies for citizens are sourced from Heaven and also through member support for one another. This takes away self-dependency; therefore pressure and fear from the citizens.

- *"So do not worry, saying, 'What shall we eat?' or 'What shall we drink?' or 'What shall we wear?' For the pagans run after all these things, and your heavenly Father knows that you need them. But seek first his kingdom and his righteousness, and all these things will be given to you as well."* (Matt. 6:31–33)

The Economic Structure

According to Jesus, all our actions are motivated by either the pursuit of money or service to God. There is no middle ground.

- *"No one can serve two masters. Either you will hate the one and love the other, or you will be devoted to the one and despise the other. You cannot serve both God and money."* (Matt. 6:24)

The economic system of worldly governments such as democracy is capitalism. This fear of scarcity motivated economic structure conditions people to get as much as they can at the expense of others. It is the cause of the wide gap between the rich and the poor in our societies and the source of greed.

The economic structure of the Kingdom government of God is commonwealth. It operates on a principle of access. Citizens have access to everything but own nothing, so it is easy for them to share their possessions. God who is the King is rightfully acknowledged as the owner of everything. For a citizen to claim ownership of something in the Kingdom of God is to contest for God's position as King and Lord. People with ownership mentality cannot inherit the Kingdom of God (see Matt 19:16-26). Because of this the evil that grows out of the love for money is plucked out as citizens direct their love to God and people. Citizens, who are a spiritual family by relationship, spread the wealth of the Kingdom by sharing what we have with the poor and needy.

- *All the believers were together and had everything in common. They sold property and possessions to give to anyone who had need. Every day they continued to meet together in the temple courts. They broke bread in their homes and ate together with glad and sincere hearts. (Acts 2:44–46)*

Provision of Healthcare

Healthcare is one of the major provisions that every government makes available to citizens.

Millions of dollars of taxpayer's money is invested into research for medicine as the sole source of treatment of diseases by worldly governments. While some medicines are effective, some only help manage the diseases, not necessarily cure it; and others have side effects that creates further problems for the body.

The method of healthcare supply in the Kingdom government of God is by the hands-on healing prayer of faith. Every disciple of Christ and citizen of God's Kingdom is entitled to divine health and equipped to pray for the healing of the sick.

- *He said, "If you listen carefully to the Lord your God and do what is right in his eyes, if you pay attention to his commands and keep all his decrees, I will not bring on you any of the diseases I brought on the Egyptians, for I am the Lord, who heals you." (Exo. 15:26)*

- *Heal the sick, raise the dead, cleanse those who have leprosy, drive out demons. Freely you have received; freely give. (Matt 10:8)*

- *Is anyone among you sick? Let them call the elders of the church to pray over them and anoint them with oil in the name of the Lord. And the prayer offered in faith will make the sick person well; the Lord will raise them up. If they have sinned, they will be forgiven. (James 5:14–15)*

Provision of Security/Defense

It is the duty of government to protect its citizens. In worldly governments, this is achieved by a provision of an army of people specially trained with weapons of war for combat in the case of a threat to the nation. The universal principle of sowing and reaping works against this strategy.

- *"Put your sword back in its place," Jesus said to him, "for all who draw the sword will die by the sword." (Matt 26:52)*

In the Kingdom government of God, angels are assigned for the defense and protection of citizens. There is no human army trained for war. Our wrestle is not against flesh and blood (see Eph. 6:12). Citizens' only fight is the fight of faith, which puts angels to work on our behalf.

- *"Now when Joshua was near Jericho, he looked up and saw a man standing in front of him with a drawn sword in his hand. Joshua went up to him and asked, "Are you for us or for our enemies?" 14"Neither," he replied, "but as commander of the army of the Lord I have now come." Then*

Joshua fell facedown to the ground in reverence, and asked him, "What message does my Lord have for his servant?" 15The commander of the Lord's army replied, 'Take off your sandals, for the place where you are standing is holy.' And Joshua did so". (Josh 5:13-15)

- *"Do you think I cannot call on my Father, and he will at once put at my disposal more than twelve legions of angels?" (Matt. 26:53)*

- *Suddenly an angel of the Lord appeared and a light shone in the cell. He struck Peter on the side and woke him up. "Quick, get up!" he said, and the chains fell off Peter's wrists. (Acts 12:7).*

- *Are not all angels ministering spirits sent to serve those who will inherit salvation? (Heb. 1:14)*

Duration or Extent of Government

The authority of worldly governments over their citizens is limited to the lifetime of citizens on earth.

The authority of the kingdom government of God over citizens is present during and after life on earth.

- *For this very reason, Christ died and returned to life so that he might be the Lord of both the dead and the living. (Rom. 14:9)*

System of Contribution

Every government must have a source for the supply of resources. Because there is no external source for provision in worldly governments, all citizens are compelled to contribute in the form of taxes for the provision of resources.

In the Kingdom government of Heaven, God is acknowledged as the Source. Citizens have the understanding that God owns everything so they allow free-flowing of resources within and outside the community (church). Citizens give to the poor and any course that contributes to God's Kingdom on earth. The motive for giving is more important that what is given.

- *If anyone is poor among your fellow Israelites in any of the towns of the land the Lord your God is giving you, do not be hardhearted or tightfisted toward them. Rather, be openhanded and freely lend them whatever they need. (Deut. 15:7-8)*

- *John answered, "Anyone who has two shirts should share with the one who has none, and anyone who has food should do the same." (Luke 3:11)*

- *Each of you should give what you have decided in your heart to give, not reluctantly or under compulsion, for God loves a cheerful giver. (2 Cor. 9:7)*

Also, the universal principle of sowing and reaping is activated when citizens of His Kingdom give, enabling God's blessings on His people. (See 2 Cor. 9:6.)

Priority of Citizens

Citizens in worldly governments are compelled to prioritize their needs and wants over anything else. The reason is, the system of government looks to the people as source.

The focus of citizens in the kingdom government of God is obedience to the King because He takes care of our needs.

- *"So do not worry, saying, 'What shall we eat?' or 'What shall we drink?' or 'What shall we wear?' For the pagans run after all these things, and your heavenly Father knows that you need them. But seek first his kingdom and his righteousness, and all these things will be given to you as well." (Matt. 6:31–33)*

THE CONCLUSION

I had the opportunity to benefit from the Christian life experiences of two very important and honest people on different occasions. Rob, who is an associate pastor, was very sad to share that his Christian life experience over the years had been somewhat disappointing. He had dedicated over 40 years to evangelism and other ministry but saw little or no change in people he thought were "saved." The other, a Catholic priest, was also sad to share how he has witnessed many graduates from Catholic schools become atheists over the years. Obviously other Christians may have positive experiences, but research carried out in one of the cities in America also testifies to the truth that Christianity as a religion does not impact the culture of a society. In most cases, the cities with most churches are also ones with the highest rates of crime, drugs, alcohol consumption, etc. As hard as it is to believe, most countries that wave the banner of Christianity fall in the category of moral breakdown.

The Church Is a Kingdom Government Not a Religion

Jesus preached the Kingdom of God and instituted the Church in the context of a Kingdom government, not as a religion. The apostles understood the message and became threats to the governments of the day. They preached Jesus as the King with a kingdom that operates by laws and principles different from the pagan societies and demonstrated the superior power of the Kingdom of Heaven. If God's answer to a broken world is the institution of the Church through Christ, then He surely expects the Church to do more than patch up and camouflage societal issues, which in many cases have instead penetrated the Church. The fact is, government is the most influential force on the culture of a society, and God's solution to our social ills was none other than His own Kingdom government through the Church.

- *But when they did not find them, they dragged Jason and some other believers before the city officials, shouting: "These men who have caused trouble all over the world have now come here, and Jason has welcomed them into his house. They are all defying Caesar's decrees, saying that there is another king, one called Jesus." (Acts 17:6–7)*

God's ultimate purpose in this age is to establish His Kingdom government on earth. Democracy, Communism, or any other system of government is simply a representation of the collective will of men. The result is injustice, fear, war, confusion, violence, crime, hatred, poverty, sicknesses and death that dominate our present world.

- *"There is a way which seemeth right unto a man, but the end thereof are the ways of death." (Prov. 14:12)*

The Will of Men Is the Mind of Satan

When Jesus referred to Peter as Satan and a stumbling block (see Matt. 16:23), it was because He said Peter's mind was set on the things of man and not of God. This tells us that any agenda that is not in line with the will of God is driven by Satan.

Believers cannot keep trusting and participating in these systems of government created by men. We are to operate independently of them. The Kingdom government of Heaven is God's invitation to the world. We are commanded by Jesus to go into the world and invite them over into His Kingdom government. The instruction is not to climb up the ladder of their system to change it, because the people that lift you up in their system also have the power to bring you down. Our mission is first to be clear on the Kingdom governing systems of God and then disciple the people of the world into it.

God did not attempt to use the children of Israel to change the governing system in Egypt but rather He delivered them from it into His own government. God's objective is to raise a community of people whose culture is founded on His government, so that they will bear fruits and attract the world around them. When the early Church rightfully represented the Kingdom government of Heaven, it records that the Lord added to their number daily (see Acts 2:47). The Kingdom of heaven therefore has its own King (Jesus), society, economy (Commonwealth), culture, health care system (healing), constitution (Bible), laws, principles, privileges, army (angels), ambassadors, etc. All these aspects of the Kingdom need to be preached to completely relieve people from the worldly systems.

Is this to say that we completely abstain from the world?

No, the objective according to the great commission is to deliver people from the worldly systems, disciple them in the governing systems of the Kingdom and discharge them back into the world, this time to be a light in the midst darkness as they apply Kingdom principles in their lives and spheres of influence. It is important for us to know that our objective for being in the world in the first place is to deliver people from the worldly governing systems into the governing system of God's Kingdom.

Are you in a religious or a Kingdom government church?

In the past, the religious church led people to Christ but failed to present the new order of life and system of the Kingdom government of Heaven. This meant that though the members had given their lives to Christ, they still had to participate in and depend on the worldly systems of government. Compromising the faith was the inevitable consequence.

The focus of a kingdom church must not only be on soul winning but also help new converts to completely dissociate from depending on or participating in worldly systems.

A religious church may specialize in only one of the following: salvation, healing, prosperity, deliverance, Holy Ghost, etc., apart from the kingdom. A Kingdom Church addresses all the needs of humanity. The gospel of the Kingdom is the only real practical solution to the needs of humanity, not just material but emotional and spiritual needs.

Jesus said that His Kingdom is not of this world, meaning the guidelines and regulations of His government are not according to the pattern of worldly governing systems. A religious church makes the worldly government's agenda its perspective and its orientation. A Kingdom Church, on the other hand, sources its agenda, perspective, and orientation according to the pattern of the Kingdom government of Heaven.

Our perception of Jesus has a lot to do with our relationship and faith in Him. A religious church perceives Jesus only as God or the Son of God. A Kingdom Church realizes the importance of seeing Jesus as a King, one who doesn't just supply their needs but one worthy of their obedience. In Luke 7:8, we see that the only other person Jesus commended on having great faith was a person who was an official of the Roman kingdom government. He clearly understood Jesus' message therefore had the right perception of Him as a King. Many of the Israelites referred to Jesus as Lord because He met their needs, but they refused to obey Him because they lacked the true revelation of Him as the King (Messiah, the Christ). Jesus clearly drew a line between the religious and Kingdom citizens by saying only those who have the true revelation of Him as the King and therefore obey Him will enter the Kingdom of Heaven, not the religious who refer to Him as Lord, because of what they can gain. (see Matt 7:21)

Key Statements

- ❖ There is a difference between the phrases the Kingdom of God and the Kingdom of Heaven.

- ❖ The Kingdom of God is God's government over the life of an individual who has accepted Jesus as Lord and lives by His principles. In the Kingdom of God, the internal world of man is conquered by Christ.

❖ The Kingdom of Heaven refers to the fellowship or community of believers and the sharing of their lives according to the principles laid by the King Jesus. In the Kingdom government of Heaven, the external world is conquered by Christ through the lifestyle of believers.

❖ Jesus is acknowledged as King when we interpret and, through His empowerment, obey His laws and principles.

❖ The Kingdom government of Heaven is simply a function of God's laws and principles perfected by Jesus in the gospels.

❖ Jesus assured us that wherever two or three meet in His name He is there. The Kingdom of Heaven is present wherever the King is.

❖ The gathering of believers (the Church), regardless of number, is equipped by God to operate and represent His Kingdom government on earth.

❖ The role of a government is to enhance peaceful coexistence and manage the wise use of resources for the benefit of all citizens.

❖ In the Kingdom government of God, God has empowered us to obey His relational laws and God seeks to manage the resources of the earth for the benefit of all citizens through His Church.

❖ Healthcare and defense, which are the main provisions by governments to their citizens, are met by God through healing and supernatural angelic protection by faith.

❖ The provision of needs by the Kingdom government of Heaven can be through supernatural provision by faith and also through the community of believers as they support one another on the basis of the Lordship of Christ (Commonwealth).

Final Thoughts

• *Cursed is the one who trusts in man, who draws strength from mere flesh and whose heart turns away from the LORD. (Jer. 17:5)*

Political campaigns are often filled with promises to meet our needs such as provide employment, better healthcare and a healthier economy, etc. Worldly governments have always strive to position themselves to provide solutions to our problems; however, many of us have been let down by them. They present enticing policies to win our hearts and our votes, but end up doing the exact opposite of what they've promised prior to elections. Most of us are left in a state of shock wondering why and how. Well, the above scripture could not make it any clearer; they are men. Man's decisions are subject to varying circumstances. They make decisions based on available facts, so when the facts change, their decisions change along with it.

One of the most political statements of the Bible was made by King Jesus in Matthew's gospel (see Matt. 6:31–33). King Jesus completely removed all dependency on worldly governments (Men) to meet our needs by saying that once we make His government (Kingdom) a priority, all the needs that worldly governments entice us with, but fail to provide, will be added to us.

Throughout history we have seen the incapability and failures as men try to do what only God does best. Man was never designed to govern without the authority and sovereign Word of God. The Word that created the earth is that "Word" that can sustain it.

Again, Romans 13 only applies to a righteous government that enforces the will of God, not a government that makes laws against God's Word. "…we must obey God rather than men" (Acts 5:29). The commission is clear: we are to disciple nations, not just individuals (Matt. 28:19). The nations are our inheritance (Ps. 2:8). Righteousness, justice, and peace are only attainable in God's Kingdom government represented in the true Church. The wisdom of God, which is what we need to resolve the issues of this world, is foolishness to worldly government authorities because they lack the Spirit of God (see 1 Cor 2:14). God's wisdom can only be revealed through His Church (see Eph. 3:10).

It is useful to note that when two different species are bred, their offspring is usually sterile. For example, a cross between a donkey and a horse produces a sterile mule that is incapable of reproducing. God cautions against mixture.

- *Do not plant two kinds of seed in your vineyard; if you do, not only the crops you plant but also the fruit of the vineyard will be defiled. (Deut. 22:9)*

The Church is warned against participation and dependence on any worldly governing system, whether it is politics, entertainment, economic, etc. We have our own system structured according to the pattern in Heaven. Our duty is to renew our minds, disconnect from the world's systems, and activate the Kingdom governing systems of Heaven here on earth. We are to "stand out" from the world, not to merge into it. Paul the apostle puts it this way:

- *Do not conform to the pattern of this world, but be transformed by the renewing of your mind. Then you will be able to test and approve what God's will is—his good, pleasing and perfect will. (Rom. 12:2)*

It is time for the Church to make preparations for the coming of our Lord. It is time for the Church, regardless of denomination, to rise up to the task and function as a Kingdom government of Heaven. It is time to take this message of the Kingdom government of God to the ends of the earth.

Every gathering of believers, however many, has two responsibilities:

- The first is to function as a Kingdom government of Heaven, independent of the world's systems.

- The second is to influence and lead people out of the worldly governing systems into the Kingdom government of Heaven.

A small, lit candle conquers a room that is full of pitch darkness. A small spoon of salt greatly affects a big bowl of soup. Size is not a problem as long as we are functioning as we are supposed to, being the light and salt of the earth. Whether we agree or not, that's where we are headed: "…of the increase of His God's Government there will be no end". The dwelling of God will be with His people.

- *Then said he, unto what is the kingdom of God like? And whereunto shall I resemble it? It is like a grain of mustard seed, which a man took, and cast into his garden; and it grew, and waxed a great tree; and the fowls of the air lodged in the branches of it. And again he said, whereunto shall I liken the kingdom of God? It is like leaven, which a woman took and hid in three measures of meal, till the whole was leavened. (Luke 13:18–21, KJV)*

How to contact the Author:

Email your questions and comments to the author at:

kingdomgoverning@gmail.com

For more study resources please visit,

Facebook - 2 Mins Weekly Word of Wisdom - Kingdom governing

Youtube Channel - kingdom governing

Website - www.kingdomgoverning.com

www.ingramcontent.com/pod-product-compliance
Lightning Source LLC
Chambersburg PA
CBHW071437090426
42737CB00011B/1684